TEACH YOURSELF

SPEAKING
ON SPECIAL OCCASIONS

Roger Mason

GW00702399

Hodder & Stoughton

A MEMBER OF THE HODDER HEADLINE GROUP

ISBN 0 340 64354 4

First published 1996
Impression number   10 9 8   7 6   5 4   3 2
Year   1999 1998 1997 1996

Typeset by Transet Limited, Coventry, England.
Printed in Great Britain for Hodder & Stoughton Educational, a division of
Hodder Headline plc, 338 Euston Road, London NW1 3BH by Cox & Wyman,
Reading, Berks.

CONTENTS

INTRODUCTION

The ability to deliver a really good speech is highly valued but only a few do it very well. More do merely an adequate job. Unfortunately many do it badly and many more cannot bring themselves to even try, avoiding the challenge at all costs. This is a great shame because nearly everyone can learn to deliver a good speech. Some, if they would only have a go, would discover that they had great talent. It is not true that only extroverts make good public speakers. Many great speakers are introverts, and frightened introverts at that.

This book should help you enormously, but do not forget that public speaking is a practical subject. A good analogy is driving a car. A lot can be learned from books but practice in driving is essential.

You are advised to get a lot of practice in public speaking. Take opportunities whenever possible to give short talks to small groups. This way you will build up your ability to make a really important speech later. Fortunately, there is a highly recommended way that this can be done. You can join one of the clubs of Toastmasters International or of the Association of Speakers Clubs. I developed my own public speaking skills as a member of a Toastmasters Club. Contact details are given in the appendix to this book.

In a Toastmasters Club (and also in a Speakers Club) you develop your skills in a planned programme. Other members are doing the same. You support each other and provide an audience for each other. It does not matter if you do badly or even dry up completely. You just learn from the experience and do better next time.

The way to get the best value from this book is to read most of it, or preferably all of it. In particular you should read the first seven chapters which give the general ground rules for speaking effectively. Only having done this should you go to a chapter that specially interests you. Of course many people will not take the time to do this.

They will get some benefit but not nearly as much. The fact that you are reading this introduction shows that you are likely to be in the wise group.

The book contains many specimen speeches. They illustrate the sorts of speech appropriate for special occasions and are designed to give you ideas to develop your own speeches.

The style of the specimen speeches in this book differs from that of most specimen speeches in books on public speaking, which usually present very unexceptional speeches with gaps saying such things as 'insert name' and 'insert details of anniversary'. The idea of this is to give something that can be used word for word and they are all-purpose, all things to all people, speeches. No one would particularly dislike the speeches, but on the other hand no one would particularly like or remember them either. Furthermore, they will not be personal to the speaker and this may show in the delivery.

The speeches in this book are not like that. They are real speeches that I might give, although in some cases fictitious circumstances have been assumed. You are encouraged to use these speeches as a starting point and to plunder them for ideas. You may well think that you know better jokes and you may be right. A personal speech written by you is likely to be more effective on the day. Nevertheless, the speeches are there for you to use. Take as much or as little as you want.

I have generally assumed the male gender throughout the book. This is not politically correct but it does avoid the unwieldy 'he or she' in hundreds of separate places. Please be assured that this book is equally intended for women speakers.

Finally, special occasions deserve special speeches. Everyone associated with this book wishes you all the best in achieving them.

1

CONTROLLING NERVES AND BUILDING CONFIDENCE

It is quite normal to be scared at the prospect of speaking in public. Millions of people share this fear. Surveys show that public speaking is feared more than sickness, flying, a visit to the dentist and many of life's other daunting experiences. For most it is a task approached with some degree of apprehension. For a few it is worse than this and it can, for a time, put a cloud over their whole lives. This is a shame because some do it extremely well. Numerous others do it competently and approach a forthcoming speech in a businesslike manner, regarding it as a job that has to be accomplished.

Nearly everyone is capable of preparing and delivering a good speech. Some would be able to communicate brilliantly if they put their minds to it and could summon up the confidence to have a go. Virtually all good speakers will acknowledge that they were nervous when delivering their early speeches. Some will admit that they avoided it and only discovered their talent after years of dodging opportunities to speak.

You may well be approaching public speaking with some degree of apprehension. This is natural, understandable and to a certain extent it is desirable. Before progressing to the rest of this book, take a few minutes to consider five reasons for thinking that you will do it well. They are all true and may not all have occurred to you.

1 Others Have Confidence In You

Some speeches are given because it is expected. An example is one of the toasts at a wedding reception, which custom dictates should be proposed by the bride's father. As the bride only has one father it is quite clear where the responsibility lies. Nevertheless, such requirements are in a minority. In most cases you will be speaking because someone has chosen you and asked you to do it. Someone thinks that you are a good person to make the speech. If this was not the case you would not have been asked. It may well be important to the person that you do well and he or she is likely to have made a shrewd assessment before issuing the invitation.

2 You Have Time To Prepare

It is rare to be asked to give an impromptu speech, and of course this cannot worry you in advance because you will not know that it is going to happen. It is much more common to have notice of days, weeks, or even months. You will normally have time to do all the necessary preparation.

3 You Only Need A Limited Amount Of Material

Inexperienced speakers often greatly overestimate the amount of material that will be needed for a speech of a given length. This can either result in some of the material not being used, or the speech being longer than intended. Both possibilities should be avoided and advice on this is given later in the book.

The most effective speeches do not contain a mass of detail, just a few points logically developed and well presented. Beginners may be pleasantly surprised at how little time they need to spend gathering basic facts and material. This frees more time for other aspects of preparation.

4 You May Well Be The Expert

Everyone is an expert in some matters. Your expertise may well be the principal reason that you have been asked to speak. This alone is a reason for confidence.

5 Nerves Can Be Made To Work To Your Advantage

Consider two athletes in the starting blocks for a race. One is tense and full of *controlled* nervous energy as he waits for the starting gun. The other feels no tension at all. The first athlete is much more likely to give his best performance and to win the race. There are similarities with public speaking and the best speech is likely to be given by a speaker who approaches the task in a state of *controlled* tension.

Even extreme nerves and physical discomfort need not be a bar to successful public speaking. This has been demonstrated on numerous occasions, a notable example being the British Prime

Minister William Pitt the Younger. He dominated the House of Commons for twenty years but always felt petrified before speaking. The fear was sometimes so bad that he would be physically sick before entering the chamber.

I have personal experience of the phenomenon. Some years ago I was involved in a civil legal action in the United States and was represented by an American lawyer in a New York court. Her preparation of the case was impressive but as the hearing approached she exhibited increasing nervousness. We travelled to the courtroom by taxi and she left her handbag in the taxi. There was an hour to wait at the courtroom before the case was called and she spent most of it in the ladies' room. With fifteen minutes to go she implored me to remove her from the case and let one of her colleagues present it. I refused this request and was rewarded by a superb courtroom performance.

The following suggestions should help you conquer, or perhaps better still, control nervousness about speaking in public.

1 Acquire Experience
The first, and most important suggestion, is simply to **do it**. There is no substitute for experience and confidence will come with practice. The first time is the worst, so get that first time out of the way and then do it frequently.

You will find opportunities. Many church groups encourage spontaneous or semi-spontaneous testimonies and prayers. They also look for help with readings, sermons, and leading a service. Resolve to make a contribution at business meetings and committee meetings. Even if it is only a few seconds long, it increases experience and boosts confidence. It will probably help the organisation too. Often the people with the most valuable comment to make are hesitant about speaking.

A vote of thanks is so often proposed badly, or not at all. Offer your services, or just do it if it is clear that it is going by default. So long as it is not too long it will probably be gratefully received. Organisations such as Rotary, Round Table and Young Farmers encourage their members to speak out.

The introduction to this book gave information and advice about joining one of the clubs of Toastmasters International, or of the Association of Speakers Clubs. It is well worth considering and you will find contact details in the appendix at the end of the book. You will experience a planned development programme, and membership gives you many chances to speak among friends. Some of these will be beginners and it does not matter if you dry up again and again. The cost is reasonable.

2 Indulge Your Superstitions

Many people (including myself) are not at all superstitious. However, feel free to do whatever makes you feel at ease. Many great performers always follow certain rituals. To take an example from an unrelated field, Stirling Moss always asked to race a car carrying his lucky number seven. Must you have a blue handkerchief and carry a lucky charm? Fine! Do it. No one will know and it will help you.

3 Feel Comfortable About Yourself

You will minimise nervousness if you feel comfortable about yourself and your appearance. Only eat and drink in moderation prior to speaking. It could dull your senses and cause you to perspire. You should be dressed appropriately for the occasion and the audience.

4 Be Well Prepared

You will feel at ease if you have done your homework, prepared well, and carry suitable notes. Later chapters tell you how to achieve all these things. If necessary you should familiarise yourself with the room, any equipment, and, most importantly, any microphone.

5 Plan A First-Class Start

Many good speeches are not memorised, still fewer read. However, an exception should be made for the first two or three sentences. The opening is the place to put a piece of your very best material and you should be word perfect with it. However, you should not read the opening.

Your confidence is bound to be boosted by an early roar of laughter or gasp of astonishment, assuming, of course, that these are the intended audience responses.

6 Take Deep Breaths

The worst time for tension is likely to be the period immediately before you are called to speak. Try a series of deep breaths, with pauses before releasing the air. It really does help and it can be done whilst wearing a fixed smile. Try it and see.

7 Do Not Let On

You may have received advice to admit to your audience that you are nervous, engage their sympathy and get them on your side. This can work, but it looks weak and it is not generally recommended. You will probably be your own worst critic and if you are nervous the audience may not realise it.

Even extreme nerves may not show or may not appear to be a serious problem. Try and look confident and do not draw attention to your nervousness. If you do not let on, the audience may never know.

SUMMARY

1 Recognise that nerves are normal, very common, and not a bar to good speaking.
2 Think positively! Study the five reasons why you should have confidence.
3 Take every opportunity to acquire experience.
4 Follow the advice to feel good as you rise to your feet.
5 Thoroughly prepare your speech and plan for a flying start.
6 Do not let the audience know that you are nervous.

2

FIRST STEPS IN PREPARING A GOOD SPEECH

There is no substitute for thorough preparation, particularly for an inexperienced speaker. Good speeches do not just happen, they are made to happen. It is a cliché but good speakers will tell you that often a great deal of work goes into their best spontaneous speeches. This chapter and the next three take you through all the stages of researching your speech and preparing it.

Decide the objectives

If you decide what you want to achieve, and how you are going to achieve it, you are much more likely to be successful. For example, an evangelical Christian will probably speak with the purpose of converting the listeners. Anything else is incidental and should not detract from this overriding objective. He will set his own aims concerning timing, but might do well to remember John Wesley's reported remark that anyone not converted in the first ten minutes would have to wait for another day.

It is you who will be speaking and it is therefore you who will decide what your objectives are. These may or may not be identical to the objectives of the person or group who asked you to speak. Perhaps the group issuing the invitation just wish to spend an interesting half hour. You can accommodate their wish whilst pursuing your aim of advocating a particular cause.

Sometimes your primary objective will be to promote a particular idea.

This could happen when you have been asked to speak about a charity and its need for funds. On such an occasion you will have very firm objectives that you want to achieve. They could be, for example, one hundred people familiar with the work of the charity, and a cheque for a significant donation at the end of the evening.

—— Consider the audience ——

Perhaps you are in charge of the event and can fairly expect to set the agenda. The bride's father may well be paying for a traditional wedding, so he may be excused for thinking that he can say what he likes and speak for as long as he likes. Nevertheless, his speech is more likely to be well received if he considers his listeners. He might usefully ponder the following:

- How much time is available? Perhaps time is short and the room has to be vacated at a certain hour. In these circumstances even very good speakers should be brief.
- What is the composition of the audience? Does everyone get along well together? At many weddings this is highly improbable. Are there people who would be offended by off-colour jokes? This is likely to be the case in a mixed-age, mixed-sex, mixed–family wedding group.
- What will please the bride and groom? It is their day after all and this question should perhaps be of first importance. They probably will not want to sit through embarrassing recollections concerning the bride's childhood.

If you are well known or have the reputation of being a good speaker, you may just be invited to speak to a group. The same thing may happen if you hold a respected position. The invitation will usually be issued in the hope that you will be entertaining.

It is good tactics and good manners to find out something about the group. You may ask for the likely number of the audience and something about them. It will also help to know one or two names and personal details.

The use of names and appropriate personal details may add to your speech and is likely to be appreciated. The audience will, correctly, think that you have taken the trouble to relate the speech to their group and are not just delivering your standard presentation. For example, the following would be a sincere and very effective opening to a talk on road safety.

> ❝ Road safety is important to all of us. But for two people in this room it is absolutely crucial. Jennifer Smith and Judy Jones both live in London Road and they have both got small children. We all know that there is no pedestrian crossing in London Road and we all know the speed at which some of the traffic moves. ❞

If you do not know enough about your prospective audience, take a little time and find out.

How to select the best timing for your speech

This is very important indeed and the starting point is to enquire for how long your hosts wish you to speak. This can be surprisingly difficult to ascertain, and you may get the response that whatever you want is fine with them. This sounds comforting but it may not be true, as you will discover if you speak for an hour when they only wanted twenty minutes.

It is therefore worth pursuing the point. It really is important that the target time selected is the most appropriate. My advice is that if in doubt, it is better to make it slightly shorter. I emphasise that I mean *slightly* shorter, not much shorter. Why do I say this? Well ... how many times have you heard it said that a speech was too long? and how many times have you heard it said that a speech was too short?

How to achieve the intended timing

Inexperienced speakers often overestimate the amount of material that will be needed for a speech of a given length. The speech will be delivered at only a fraction of the speed at which the same words could be read.

In the course of a minute you could probably read about 360 of the words in this book. However, reading aloud you would probably get through about 190 words. Now imagine a speech with its pauses for effect, its quotations, its emphasis on special passages, and hopefully the pauses for laughter and other audience reaction. Depending on speaking style you will probably deliver between 85 and 115 words a minute. So for a typical five-minute speech you will need between 425 and 575 words.

You should prove this for yourself. Start by reading for exactly a minute then counting the words that you have read. Then read the same passage aloud and see how long it takes. Finally deliver it as though to an audience. Emphasise the parts that you think are important. Stop occasionally and look round the room. Stop sometimes to accommodate possible laughter.

If you prepare your speech word for word, with the intention of memorising it, you can plan the time very accurately. If it has 500 words, and your delivery style averages 100 words a minute, you should be close to five minutes. If you prepare headline notes it is not quite so easy but you should still be able to plan quite closely.

When the speech is delivered it may be desirable, or necessary, to alter the timing slightly. Perhaps the event is running late, or the previous speakers have taken longer than planned. Perhaps the audience is showing signs of restlessness. In these circumstances you may not want to speak for as long as originally planned. More unusually there may be circumstances in which you want to speak for slightly longer than intended.

The desired flexibility can be achieved by preparing a speech slightly longer than you think will be needed. It is likely that your opening and conclusion are absolutely essential. In between may be a number of freestanding points.

Let us assume that you have been asked to speak for about 10 minutes, and that your opening and conclusion will each last for about ninety seconds. If you prepare nine points of one minute each you have a speech that should last for twelve minutes. If points six, seven, eight and nine stand alone they can be included or omitted according to a decision made at the time. You will then have a speech that could last between eight and twelve minutes.

An example of a speech that lends itself to this approach is one that puts forward a number of arguments for doing something, such as voting in a particular way. You should clearly mark your notes to show the section that may be discarded, and your best material should of course be in the section that is sure to be used. Do make certain that the exclusion of a point does not weaken the construction of the speech as a whole.

Watch the time as you deliver the speech

There is a separate chapter giving advice on the delivery of your speech. But it is worth mentioning at this point that unless the speech is very short you should be aware of elapsed time as you deliver it. It may be a good idea to have a timer or watch in your sight, but not obvious to the audience. It is not a good idea to keep glancing at a watch on your wrist as you speak.

SUMMARY

1 Thorough preparation is important. Success depends on it.
2 Be clear about your own objectives.
3 Think about the audience in advance of the speech.
4 If necessary ask questions in advance, about the audience and about the event.
5 Timing the speech is important. Take it seriously.
6 Work out your personal words per minute delivery rate.
7 Plan your speech to achieve the desired time. Build in some flexibility.
8 Watch timing as you deliver the speech.

3

ENSURE THAT YOUR SPEECH IS SOUNDLY CONSTRUCTED

In the last chapter you were advised to start by deciding on your objectives, gathering information about the occasion if necessary, and deciding your planned speech time. You will now be ready to construct your speech in detail, and this means putting your thoughts on paper.

—— Put something on paper ——

It is usually best to get something on paper as quickly as possible. Some people find it difficult to get started but sound advice is to **just do it**. Get something on paper. Get anything on paper. No matter how badly it is done, this is the starting point. You can then keep amending it until you get it right.

Put down thoughts as they occur to you. Put them down in no particular order, and have too many rather than too few. At this stage you are not preparing the speech in detail so there is no need for complete sentences, just phrases and single words. Thoughts can come at any time, so you might like to keep a piece of paper in your pocket and make a note as ideas occur to you.

You will need to add points, delete points, amend points, and juggle the order of the points. This leads to having the speech in outline, all in words and phrases. You are then ready to prepare the speech in detail, putting in the humour, the anecdotes, and everything else that will make the speech special.

Construct the speech

There are several ways of constructing a speech but the most common is the so-called sandwich construction. It is so named because the opening and closing are like the two pieces of bread. The solid content of the speech is the meat in the middle. We will consider the three parts in turn.

The opening

The first 30 seconds are the most important of the whole speech. You will not get a second chance to make a good first impression. In this time you have to get the audience's attention and make it believe that your speech will be worth listening to. The position can be retrieved if you fail, but it will be an uphill struggle.

If the audience is inattentive you must make them focus on you. If it is attentive you must keep that attention, consolidate your position, and make then think that it is worth concentrating in order to get the full benefit of what you are about to say.

The opening of the speech is the place to put some of your very strongest material. If you start with a joke, make it your best, and preferably short. Whatever else you do, you must get attention for yourself, but it should be done in a way that is relevant to your purpose and the content that is to follow. You could certainly get attention by shouting an obscene word but it would not be a wise thing to do. It would not be the right sort of attention, nor would it be the sort to make the audience give a good hearing to the rest of your speech.

The opening should lead smoothly into the main part of the speech. It should be effective in its own right but there should be a connection with what is to follow.

The following suggestions illustrate nine effective ways of getting attention and getting your speech off to a strong start.

A dramatic statement

This challenges the audience to take note of the power of what you are saying. Two examples are:

❛ Last month two children were killed by their parents within five miles of this room. ❜

and

❛ It is quicker to drive from Birmingham to the edge of London than it is to drive the last ten miles to the centre of the city. ❜

An interesting statement

There are countless possibilities, the key being that it must be absolutely fascinating to the particular audience. A speech on ancient Egyptian civilisation could effectively start as follows:

❛ The Great Pyramid of Cheops was finished in 2580 BC. It remained the world's tallest man-made structure until the completion of Lincoln Cathedral in AD 1548. ❜

An interesting start to a speech on British railways would be:

❛ The Box Tunnel on the Great Western Railway was Brunel's greatest achievement. The rising sun shines directly through the tunnel on only one day of the year and that day is Brunel's birthday. He swore that it was a coincidence. ❜

A question

This usually works well. You could either answer the question at once, answer it later, or leave the audience with the unanswered question. An example is:

❛ Nurses have just had a pay rise. What proportion of the extra money do you think that the government takes in tax and national insurance? Twenty per cent, twenty-five per cent, what do you think? ❜

A controversial statement

Examples are:

❛ Don Bradman was the greatest batsman that ever trod this earth. ❜

and

❛ President Harry Truman had better advisers than any president since the Second World War. ❜

A quotation

A speech advocating the banning of hunting could usefully start with:

❛ Oscar Wilde said that hunting is the pursuit of the uneatable by the unspeakable. ❜

A speech to a group of senior citizens could start with:

❛ General MacArthur remarked that old soldiers never die. They simply fade away. ❜

Something personal to the audience

A good example was given in the last chapter. It concerned the opening of a speech on road safety (see page 10).

A surprise

Most audiences would be intrigued by:

❛ America spends more on ice-cream than it does on space research. ❜

A sentimental statement

A speech promoting holidays in the Isle of Man could commence with:

❛ On a clear day it is possible to stand at the top of Snaefell mountain and see six ancient Kingdoms. They are the Kingdoms of England, Ireland, Scotland and Wales. Then there is Man itself and the Kingdom of Heaven. ❜

A joke

Humour is one of the most effective ways of starting a speech. The joke must of course really be funny. A joke that falls flat is counter productive. For best results the joke should be short, relevant, and well told.

A speech about business ethics could start:

❛ A shopkeeper was asked by his eight-year-old son to tell him what was meant by an ethical decision. After some thought he replied by giving an example: 'If a customer pays me and there are two £5 notes stuck together I have to make an ethical decision. Do I tell your mother?' ❜

The main body of the speech

Unless the speech is very short this section will take up most of the available time. It is where arguments are developed, information is imparted, and hopefully it is where you will achieve your main objectives in making the speech.

The main part of the speech will consist of a series of points. Beware of having too many points. An audience can only assimilate so much detail. The points should follow logically one from another. A few simple points, well developed, flowing, and making a cohesive whole, can make a very powerful speech. This can be better than stronger points that do not lead anywhere.

There are countless possibilities for speeches and their body and development. The following example illustrates the general points made above. One of the examples of a good opening was for a speech promoting holidays in the Isle of Man. This speech could be developed using the following main headings:

- opening
- history of the island
- tourist facilities
- hotels
- beaches
- communications
- cost of holidays
- motor cycle races
- conclusion.

The speech will benefit if the points are smoothly linked rather than stated baldly one after the other. For example the section on the cost of holidays could be smoothly linked to the section on motor cycle races in the following way:

❛ So you can see that holidays in the Isle of Man are tailored to suit all pockets, and to offer unbeatable value, and that's without even considering the T.T. motor cycle races for which the island is famous. These just have to be the greatest free show in the world. The circuit is 37 miles long and you can watch the races absolutely free from hundreds of vantage points. Sure, there are grandstands, and good value they are too, but you really can watch for absolutely nothing at all. You cannot say that about Silverstone or Indianapolis. ❜

The conclusion

It is important to finish on a strong note, leaving the audience with a definite and positive memory. Whatever the type of speech the conclusion, like the opening, is the place for some of your strongest material. The following are some of the possibilities:

By answering a question and drawing a conclusion

In the section on opening the speech an example was given of a question about the tax payable by nurses. The speech could leave the question and proceed to make all the points in the main part. It could then conclude by answering the question, perhaps in a way like this:

❛ A few minutes ago I asked you to estimate the proportion of the nurses' rise taken by the government in tax and national insurance. The answer ladies and gentlemen is shocking. It is 35 per cent. Our priorities are very, very, wrong. I rest my case. ❜

By a call to action

This is one of the most common conclusions because many speeches are made with the purpose of persuading the listeners to do something. Make it powerful and do not mind appealing to the emotions. An American political speech could conclude in the following way:

❛ This state has been very well served by its Republican Senator. Next Thursday you have the chance to vote for him again. Take that chance. Do it for your family. Do it for yourself. Vote Republican. ❜

These sentiments will of course enrage half of the American readers of this book. They can and should substitute the word 'Democratic' for the word 'Republican'.

If the hoped-for action can be taken at once, seize the moment. There will never be a better time than immediately following the speech. If it is an appeal for funds pass round the plate as you sit down. If it is an appeal for letters to be written, hand out paper and envelopes on the spot. I once gave a short talk asking forty people to fill in, and carry, kidney donor cards. Nearly everyone wanted to do it but I knew that if the matter was left only one or two would actually bother to obtain the cards. But I finished by handing out forty cards, and over thirty were filled in on the spot.

With a surprise

Tell the audience something that they did not know and the opposite of what they are expecting.

By saying something that sums up what you have said

An example is:

> ❦ So these, ladies and gentlemen, are the three greatest engineering achievements of Isambard Kingdom Brunel. Any one of them would be remarkable, but together they add up to just one word. That word is genius. ❧

With humour

Comedians know to leave them while they are laughing. It is very good indeed to sit down with laughter ringing round the room, but of course the humour must be very good to achieve this.

With a quotation

This can be effective if it is apt and sums up what has gone before. To take just one example from countless possibilities, a speech with a military theme could well conclude with a quotation from Rudyard Kipling:

> ❦ It's Tommy this, an' Tommy that,
> an' 'Chuck him out the brute',
> But it's Saviour of 'is country
> when the guns begin to shoot. ❧

Finally, remember that your conclusion must be relevant to the speech. It should be strong and it should be memorable, but especially it should be relevant. The ideal situation is to leave the audience wanting more.

SUMMARY

1 Get ideas on paper as soon as possible.
2 Keep juggling the ideas until you get it right.
3 The first thirty seconds are the most important of the whole speech.
4 You must get attention at the start. Use some of your strongest material.
5 Link your points smoothly.
6 Finish on a strong note.
7 Try and leave them wanting more.

4

MAKE YOUR SPEECH SPARKLE

Good speech construction is important, but it is not enough. You will want to put that little extra into your speech. You will want it to be more than worthy. You will want it to be special. In the words of this chapter heading, you will want it to sparkle.

Boredom is the worst enemy of the speech maker. At all costs you must avoid boring your audience. This is partly a matter of delivery and this is covered in a later chapter. But is is also a matter of content and style.

— Make your speech memorable —

There is a story, no doubt apocryphal, of a boy asked by his parents about the subject of a sermon. 'Sin' was the answer. 'What did he say about sin?' asked his parents. 'He was against it,' answered the boy, and no amount of questioning could elicit any further information. The preacher had communicated the general idea, but he had not managed to make his sermon memorable.

There is a lesson for us all and I suggest that you prove it to yourself. Think about a speech that you heard some time ago, perhaps as recently as a week or two ago. Now try and recall something about the speech. You may well not remember anything at all, but if you do it is likely to be something very funny, a scintillating phrase, a moment of emotion, or a fascinating anecdote.

This is certainly true of famous historical speeches. You will recall President Franklin Roosevelt saying 'a day that will live in infamy' and on another occasion 'we have nothing to fear except fear itself'. You may remember Sir Winston Churchill addressing the American Congress and saying 'westward look the sky is bright'.

Sprinkle your speech with humour, emotion, scintillating phrases, and anecdotes. Not too many, of course, but enough to lift it out of the ordinary. You will be much more likely to be successful on the day and your speech is much more likely to be remembered afterwards.

When you prepare your speech, you may find that time limitations make you consider dropping the humour, the anecdotes, and the other highlights. You may feel that the content is so important that everything else must go to make room for it. This is a serious mistake and on no account should you do it. These things ensure that the remaining part of your content is understood and remembered. This is much better than getting in more detail, all of which is promptly forgotten.

A speech is not the same as a written article

Great speeches frequently lose their impact when reproduced in written form. A speech may be slightly ungrammatical and it may, probably should, be delivered with long pauses for emphasis.

Phrases may be electrifying when spoken but inappropriate when written. President Abraham Lincoln commenced his Gettysburg address with the words 'Four score and seven years ago our fathers brought forth on this continent'. It is one of the most famous speeches ever made, but had it been in written form he may well have put 'This country was founded eighty-seven years ago'. Lincoln did not make the mistake of writing an article then reciting it. What he prepared was a magnificent speech.

Do keep this in mind. Always try to remember how a speech will sound. It may look good but it has got to sound good as well. Long words that are difficult to pronounce may be excellent on paper, but not a good choice for a speech.

The use of anecdotes

Nothing makes a speech sparkle more than a really good anecdote, and frequently this is the part that is most remembered. I will illustrate the truth of this with a personal story, or perhaps I should say a personal anecdote.

I once gave a speech about my view that Britain was wise to abolish capital punishment and that it would be a mistake to bring it back. This is not the general view of the British public and it was not the view of most of my audience. Most of them wanted to hang all murderers, and a few would probably have hung me as well.

The mood of the group changed when I told them that I had once thought the same way as them, and had made the point to a friend. After a long pause he had replied that he hoped that I did not want to make it retrospective or he would not be there. He explained that at the age of nineteen his grandfather had been sentenced to death for murder.

There had been one or two extenuating circumstances and the sentence had been commuted to life imprisonment. His grandfather had actually served seven years in prison. Since his release, more than half a century earlier, he had led an admirable life and was held in high regard by all who knew him. I knew this to be true. Such a change in a man might be very unusual, but it could happen, and here was the proof.

As a result the audience settled down and gave the rest of the speech a fair hearing.

The story had all the features of a good anecdote, namely:

- it was true
- it was very interesting
- it was a story personal to the speaker
- it was very relevant
- it was delivered with conviction.

It may be permissible to take a little poetic licence with anecdotes. Often the only person who can know if it is absolutely true is you, the speaker. If a point is illustrated by rearranging one or two details, then perhaps you may feel justified in doing so. Circumstances vary and you must judge the circumstances and the occasion. Obviously, you should not do it in a speech where the audience is entitled to depend on your word. My speech on capital punishment would, in my opinion, come into that category.

The use of surprise

Surprise often goes well with humour and is an excellent way of making a memorable point. There is an art in leading an audience towards expecting something, and then delivering the opposite.

Lord Lawson, the former British Chancellor of the Exchequer, was a master of this technique. On one famous occasion the country was expecting him to introduce a tax on the lump sum element of pension pay outs. In his budget speech he built up to what he referred to as the anomalous but much-loved lump sum. At the mention of this the opposition MPs started to hoot and cause general uproar. After the Speaker had managed to restore order, Lawson delighted his own party by saying that he had no proposals to introduce such a tax.

Another example of the effective use of surprise, coupled with humour, was given by a management expert lecturing on company takeovers. He made the point that invariably the most generous employee benefits became standard for the whole of the combined group. He gave as an example a company employing 700 people, all of whom received six weeks' paid holiday. It took over a company employing 200 people, all of whom received two weeks' holiday plus All Saints' Day. The result was a company employing 900 people, all of whom received six weeks' holiday. After a pause he added, 'plus All Saints' Day'.

The use of memorable phrases

These can light up a speech. Who can forget the speech in which the Prince of Wales described a building as 'a monstrous carbuncle on the face of a much-loved institution?' Certain British architects did not like it, but it made a point admirably.

Prince Charles intended the furore that 'monstrous carbuncle' caused. However, the effect may sometimes be unintended and not appreciated at the time. Harold Macmillan once made a speech at a fête in Bedford, in which he stated that most people in Britain had never had it so good. The speech passed without comment at the time but was quoted later. 'Never had it so good' helped Macmillan in the short term but became notorious for years afterwards.

Despite this, it is an excellent idea to try and include phrases that are out of the ordinary, and which illustrate a point.

Speak with authority

Authority is hard to define, but we all recognise it when we encounter it. All speakers strive to speak with authority. If it is a serious speech in which the aim is to persuade, perceived authority will lend weight. Even a more light-hearted speech will be received with close attention if an air of authority is brought to the occasion.

The speaker starts with an advantage if a favourable reputation precedes him or her. This may have been earned by prior speeches, from a general reputation, from certain achievements, or as a result of holding a certain position.

A speaker is more likely to project authority if he feels confident and at ease. This is of course easier said than done, but it goes hand in hand with sincerity. If you have persuaded yourself, you are some way towards persuading other people.

The best boost to confidence, and thus to authority, is the knowledge that you have done a thorough job in preparing the speech, and especially in checking the facts. Only you will know if this is the case. It damages credibility if an audience hears something that it knows to be incorrect, even if it is incidental to the main point.

Humour

Nearly all good speeches contain at least some humour. A few are a scream from beginning to end, but much more common is a speech illuminated by wit at key points. On many occasions an audience will be expecting humour and will be disappointed if it is not delivered.

There are few speeches that do not give an opportunity for a funny story, a witty phrase, or some other manifestation of humour. It is frequently the highlight of a speech and the part that is best remembered. It is over thirty years ago but millions still remember Nikita Khrushchev banging his shoe on the table whilst Harold Macmillan was addressing an assembly of the United Nations. Macmillan brought the house down by asking for a translation. People still recall Hubert Humphrey's witty denunciation of Barry Goldwater at the 1964 Democratic Party Convention. Tasteful humour can even be appropriate at a solemn occasion such as a funeral or memorial service. The broadcaster Brian Redhead was known to be very proud of his North of England roots and residence. At his memorial service a speaker told of him closing his radio programme with a quick summary of the weather forecast, 'bright in the north, dull in the south ... just like the people'.

Few people have the skill to be a stand up comic, so not many good speeches are delivered in this style. There is no hiding place for a comic who does not get the laughs. Unless you are gifted it is best to avoid this approach, at least at the start of your speaking career.

Wit and humour are most effective if they are relevant to the speech and flow naturally. They are not so effective if they have to be flagged **here is a joke**, or if they are irrelevant to what has passed and what is to come.

Short stories are usually more effective than longer stories, and the longer the story the better must be the punchline. Jokes should not be told that are in bad taste and which risk offending even part of the audience. Circumstances differ. What is acceptable on one occasion may not be appropriate for another. You are advised to follow a golden rule, **if in doubt, leave it out**.

—— Be sincere and be yourself ——

There are great advantages in speaking with sincerity. An audience will usually sense that a speaker is sincere and respect him or her for it. They are more likely to give a fair hearing, even if they do not agree with the views expressed. Equally, they may sense insincerity and react accordingly.

If you are being yourself and projecting your own character, the speech is more likely to project favourably. This too will be respected by the audience. Speakers being themselves are more likely to control their nerves and appear relaxed. Some observers believe that President Reagan and President Nixon illustrate the point. President Reagan projected sincerity and his character in his speeches, and as a result generally appeared to be at ease. On the other hand President Nixon often did not appear to be at ease.

———— **Your speaking style** ————

Fortunately, successful speeches can be made in a very wide variety of styles. There are of course approaches that should be avoided, and approaches that may be emulated as they are often successful. You are generally free to develop a style that suits you. In fact you should do so. It would be a dull world if everyone spoke in the same way.

SUMMARY

1 At all costs avoid boring the audience.
2 Make room for humour, anecdotes, emotion and scintillating phrases.
3 Remember that a speech must be spoken. A brilliant written article may not do.
4 A surprise can work wonders, especially when combined with humour.
5 An apt anecdote can make the speech.
6 Thorough preparation will help you speak with authority and it will boost your confidence.
7 Most audiences hope for humour. It can be used in nearly all speeches.
8 Be sincere, be yourself and develop your own style.

5

THE PREPARATION
AND USE OF NOTES

There are four basic approaches to the use of notes in delivering a speech. Each approach has advantages and disadvantages, so it is worth considering them in turn.

An extemporaneous speech

This is not prepared in advance at all and consequently no notes are available. The speech may be extemporaneous because the speaker does not know in advance that he will be speaking. On the other hand he may know but choose not to prepare, just getting to his feet and saying what comes into his mind at the time. This can work well for gifted people, but it is a high-risk strategy not recommended for beginners.

An advantage is that the speech will sound spontaneous. This is because it is spontaneous. A further advantage is that it saves the speaker the time that he would have spent in preparation. This may be the motivation for a confident and accomplished speaker.

Disadvantages are that there may be a lack of structure and a lack of detail. With hindsight the speaker may well think of things that should have been said. There is also of course the risk of drying up or a similar disaster. Someone may be offended if an important name or point is missed or muddled.

An extemporaneous speech may be acceptable for a good speaker making a short speech on a subject that he knows very well. Even in these circumstances he would probably do better if he spent a few minutes jotting down outline points.

For nearly all readers of this book this approach is not recommended.

—— A speech read from a script ——

An inexperienced speaker may be tempted to write out his speech in full and then read it word for word.

The biggest advantage is that this may make him feel confident. Also he is less likely to make an embarrassing slip of the tongue, his delivery will probably be almost word perfect, and the length will be very close to the intended time.

It is even possible to read a speech prepared by someone else. This sometimes occurs when the speaker and subject are very important. A politician delivering a major speech may come into this category, and the text will probably be issued to the press in advance. Such a speaker may have the use of an autocue which will overcome some of the disadvantages of reading a script.

All these are real advantages but you are nevertheless advised not to do it. There are powerful disadvantages and only in rare circumstances should you consider reading a speech. No matter how good the reading, it will still sound like a reading rather than a speech. The speaker will only have limited eye contact with the audience and will not sound spontaneous. He will be inhibited in establishing the all important rapport with the audience.

Over the years you will have listened to some very good and memorable speeches. Ask yourself if any of them were read. Almost certainly, none of them were.

A speech memorised from a script

This is when a speech is prepared in detail and written out word for word. It is then memorised and delivered without the use of the script. If you have a good memory, and have the time and inclination to memorise your speech, it is a very effective method. It is obviously more suitable for a short speech than a long one, but many excellent speeches are delivered in this way.

Some people are capable of prodigious feats of memory. Sir Winston Churchill used this method exclusively for many years, and all his earlier speeches were memorised. This included many speeches thirty or forty minutes long. On one tragic occasion his memory failed him in the House of Commons and he had to sit down in confusion.

The advantages of memorised speech are:

- You can deliver very carefully prepared content.
- You should achieve closeness to the desired time.
- You can establish eye contact and rapport with the audience.
- You can move about, not needing a fixed position for notes.

The disadvantages are:

- The time necessary for word for word preparation.
- The time necessary to memorise the speech.
- The possibility that a memorised speech may sound stilted in the same way as a read speech.

To overcome the last point always remember that it is a speech and not a memorised reading. Try and give it all the breaks and naturalness of a speech.

You can overcome the risk of memory loss by having the script with you, and I recommend that you should do so. However, you should intend to not use it, or only make slight use of it. You should even put the script face-down on the table or lectern, and only turn it over if it is essential to do so. You would then have the confidence of knowing that you have immediate access, without the temptation to semi-read.

If you do use this method, space your notes out well. In practice you will probably find that you can refresh your memory with only a very brief glance. It may be a good idea to mark the script for pauses, emphasis etc, and to do this in ink of a different colour.

This is one of the two recommended methods; the second method follows. A memorised presentation is particularly suitable for beginners and for short speeches.

A speech delivered from summarised notes

A speech is prepared in detail and then put into the form of summarised notes. It may first be written out word for word and then summarised into the form of headline notes. Alternatively, the speech may be prepared directly in note form and never put on to a word for word basis. The longer the speech the less likely that it will be written out word for word first.

This is a highly recommended method, especially for longer speeches. It combines the best features of the other methods. You prepare the content of the speech in detail so you get the structure and other advantages of careful preparation. On the other hand delivery of the speech can appear spontaneous and you can develop a good rapport with the audience.

An example of a speech with supporting headline notes

As well as illustrating the preparation of headline notes, the following specimen speech illustrates some of the points explained in the preceding chapters. The speech is for a hypothetical chairman of a Parent-Teacher Association, and is for delivery after the school play. It is 357 words long and should be delivered relatively slowly, with pauses for applause. It will probably last between three and four minutes.

The speech has two purposes. Firstly, it is to thank everyone who has worked on the play and secondly, it is to appeal for donations towards the cost of curtains for the school hall.

❡ What a marvellous evening. I can see from your faces that you have enjoyed it just as much as I have.

Ladies and gentlemen! I am speaking to you tonight for two reasons. The first of course is to thank everyone who has worked so hard to make tonight's play successful.

I would love to mention all the cast because they all did well, but in particular we thank Sarah Jenkins and Bryan Morris.

How did they learn all those lines with A Levels just around the corner? Sarah, Bryan, I take my hat off to both of you. Well done!

Then there are all the others who have given up their time: the group who built that splendid set, the staff in the office who sold the tickets, and all the others.

I bet you did not realise that there was a prompter in the wings. I do not think that she spoke once, but she was there. Thank you Mrs Patel.

Headmaster, year after year the school supports the annual play. We all know that without you and your staff it could not take place.

And finally the Director, Graham Matthews. This is the seventh play that Graham has produced, everything from Shakespeare to Alan Ayckbourn. And they get better each year. Well done Graham, you really are this school's Mr Drama.

Ladies and gentlemen we have once again only charged £2 for each ticket. Just enough to cover costs and no more. But I am asking you to show your appreciation in a very practical way. This hall desperately needs new curtains. They were middle-aged when I was at the school and they just will not last any longer.

The Parent-Teacher Association has pledged itself to find £6,000 to replace them, and we want to raise £500 of it tonight. Please will you help us? There are collecting plates by each door.

Thank you for your support and I hope to see you all at next year's play. Now I am sure that you will want to join me in a round of applause in appreciation of everyone involved in tonight's performance. ❯

The speech has been prepared anticipating an outstanding success. If this does not actually happen the speech will need minor modification on the night. The speaker will still want to thank everyone involved but would be advised to be less extravagant with the praise.

The speech thanks four people by name and the headmaster by title. Everyone else is thanked as part of a group. The speaker would be well advised to think about this carefully. Should anyone else be mentioned by name? Any reporter on a local newspaper will attest that this really does matter. People care passionately that their name is mentioned, and they are offended if it is not pronounced correctly. One of the main objects of the speech is to praise and thank people who have given their time. So he must get it right.

The headline notes for the specimen speech

The notes will be prepared by you to help you. There is nothing wrong in adapting the style to suit yourself. After all it is you who will be using them. That said, the speech could well be put into note form as follows:

MARVELLOUS EVENING

FIRSTLY THANK EVERYONE INVOLVED

–CAST, ESPECIALLY   SARAH JENKINS
                                     BRYAN MORRIS

– OTHERS: BUILT SET
            SOLD TICKETS
            ALL OTHERS
            PROMPTER   MRS PATEL
            HEADMASTER AND STAFF
ESPECIALLY   GRAHAM MATTHEWS
                                  MR DRAMA

ONLY CHARGED £2 PER TICKET

NEED TO RAISE £6,000 FOR CURTAINS

HOPE FOR £500 TONIGHT

ASK FOR YOUR HELP

COLLECTING PLATES AT EACH DOOR

SEE YOU NEXT YEAR

All the names in these notes are straightforward but if a name is difficult to pronounce, or is pronounced differently to the way it is written, it may be necessary to show it phonetically. For example, the former British Prime Minister could be shown thus:

❛ LORD HOME (PRONOUNCED HUME) ❜

An inexperienced speaker will probably use lengthy notes and progress to making them shorter as his or her confidence increases. There is nothing wrong with this but do avoid the temptation to semi-read the speech.

Using your notes

Your notes should be as unobtrusive as possible. You will almost certainly have seen speakers holding great sheaves of paper, perhaps even A4 or foolscap size. A lectern can hide many sins, but you may have seen a speaker folding large sheets of paper over the top. This is exactly what you must not do.

The notes are best put on pieces of card. These are better than paper because they are less likely to curl up and drop on the floor. The cards should not be too big. If there are a lot of notes it is better to have many cards of a reasonable size rather than a small number of large cards.

If you know that you have the use of a lectern you may like to use cards measuring about nine inches by five inches. These can be put on the lectern and slid from side to side as they are used. This way they are not seen by the audience. For the same reason it is best to use only one side and not turn the cards over. As you work though the speech you should leave the cards on the lectern rather than moving them off. At the end of the speech you can gather up all the cards at once and take them away.

If you do not expect to have the use of a lectern it is preferable to use smaller cards. These can be kept in the palm of your hand, and a card from the top discarded or put at the back after it has been used. Alternatively, they can be put face upwards on a table.

The writing on the cards should be large and well spaced out. You should be able to see and grasp a phrase in a second.

The most effective delivery is to refer to notes as little as possible. Failing this you should make your references as unobtrusive as possible. This may well be easier than you think. At school you probably found that copying out notes helped fix important facts in your mind. Similarly, the preparation of good notes will help fix the content of the speech in your mind. You may well find that you need hardly refer to the notes at all.

If your notes are in headline form you should aim to glance down and get an idea extremely quickly. The same applies for a speech written out in full. The more time that you are looking at the audience the better, although of course your glance must be long enough to fix an idea in your mind.

The style of your notes is up to you but perhaps a phrase in the notes will cover about thirty seconds of speaking time.

SUMMARY

1 Decide your basic approach (memorised script or headline notes).
2 If you use a full script mark it for pauses, emphasis etc.
3 If you use headline notes decide whether or not to prepare a full script first.
4 Take great care with names.
5 Put the notes on suitably sized cards.
6 Notes should be in large print and suitably spaced out.
7 The use of the notes should be as unobtrusive as possible.
8 Try and use the notes to fix an idea in your mind with a glance.

6

MASTER THE DELIVERY OF YOUR SPEECH

If you think back to your schooldays you will probably remember some teachers who had the knack of putting their subjects across. They somehow made their lessons come alive and were, by nearly all tests successful teachers. You will probably also remember some teachers whose lessons were deadly dull and not memorable. Many of them were probably very knowledgeable and hard working, and they presented meticulously constructed lessons. But, they were dull. They could not master the delivery.

There are a lot of similarities with public speaking. It is very important that your speech is well prepared, well researched, and brimming with sparkling content. But by itself this is not enough. You have got to present it on the day. This chapter contains advice on how to achieve a successful delivery.

Prior to speaking

You will give your best if you feel confident and relaxed. This desirable state of affairs is more likely to be achieved if you:

- arrive in good time
- check the room, the equipment, any props and visual aids, and any microphone
- only eat and drink in moderation prior to speaking.

—— Make a good first impression ——

In Chapter 3 you were advised that the first few sentences of your speech are extremely important, and that you would not have a second chance to make a good first impression. This is true, but the very first impression will already have been made before you open your mouth.

It may be unfair but people are judged on their appearance and their demeanour. An audience will do this subconsciously, and they will do it as you rise to your feet or walk to the speaking position. Their judgement will be based on your physical appearance, including clothes and grooming. It will also be based on your posture and the almost indefinable signals that you convey. In short, it will based on your air of authority.

You should dress appropriately for the occasion, which may not seem to be very helpful advice. It is something that has to be judged on a one by one basis, but if in doubt it is usually best to err on the side of conservative dressing. Whatever the degree of informality in dressing, care should be taken with personal grooming, shoes and so on. This is rather condescending advice and, in the case of nearly all readers, unnecessary. It is nevertheless important.

Demeanour means whether or not you look nervous, whether you stoop, whether you make furtive glances, whether you look at the floor instead of making eye contact. To sum it up in a phrase, try and look as though you are supposed to be there. Unless it is impossible, you should always speak in a standing position. Move to the speaking position, or rise to your feet, not hurriedly but in a reasonably brisk manner.

Nothing succeeds like success, and it should all come naturally as your experience increases.

—————— The use of your voice ——————

It is essential that you are heard. If you do not achieve this basic objective, and a few speakers do not, then everything else is irrelevant. You must adjust your voice according to the audience and the room. If half a dozen people are gathered in a small room, then something close to a normal conversational tone will suffice. If there is a large group of people you must raise your voice and project it.

It is rarely necessary to shout, and a speech delivered in this way is not ideal. You will normally be well heard if you raise your voice slightly, raise your head slightly, and aim to speak to all in the room.

A speech delivered in a monotone is not likely to be well received. Vary the tone and aim to achieve vocal variety. Try and express emotion with your voice. If you are saying something sad your voice, as well as your words, should let the audience know that you are sad. If you are angry as you speak, then the audience should know it from your tone. Your voice, as well as your words, should tell them that you are flaming mad and they had better know it. A lot of expression in the voice is a good thing. Most speakers have too little rather than too much.

Put pauses into your delivery. Pause to emphasise important points and pause to accommodate audience reaction. You will be hoping for audience reaction. This is true for all speeches but especially if there is humour in them. Do not stifle audience reaction when you get it. Rather, you should nurture it and pause to allow it. If you talk through a burst of laughter the audience will not be at ease. They may not laugh out loud the next time something funny is said.

Finally, a few words about the speed of delivery. There is no magical speed to be measured in words per minute. Nevertheless, nearly all good speeches are delivered more slowly than normal conversation. Some people do deliver speeches too slowly, but too quickly is considerably more common.

Good vocal skills are always important, as is promoting a general rapport with the audience. You should be particularly conscious of it if you have memorised your speech.

Eye contact

This follows from general demeanour mentioned earlier in this chapter. The human species values open, engaging eye contact, such as is normally found in a conversation between friends. It is subconsciously taken as an indication of confidence, authority and sincerity. This applies to public speaking as well as to more intimate encounters and you should strive to make it a feature of your performance.

Some speeches are made without the speaker making eye contact with the audience. This sad state of affairs can happen because the speaker's eyes are:

- looking downwards at the floor
- looking out over the top of the audience
- looking at the audience but not focusing.

These are all mistakes but each one is less bad than the one before. Worst of all is looking downwards. You should aim to look at the audience virtually the whole time. If it is a small or medium-sized group try to look at individual people, each one for a few seconds at a time. It is a mistake to concentrate too much on just one person as he or she may start to feel uncomfortable. Try to engage glances with specific individuals. This way everyone should feel included. This will not be possible if you are speaking at the Royal Albert Hall or Yankee Stadium, but the great majority of speeches are to relatively small groups. If the audience is very large you should still make a conscious effort to look at, and speak to, every section of it.

— Hand movements and gestures —

This causes a lot of problems and it is probably best to start with a list of the things that you should **not** do:

- Do not put your hands in your pockets.
- Do not put your hands rigidly at your sides or behind your back and leave them there.
- Do not whirl your hands about in a distracting manner. Magnus Pyke is an engaging television performer, but not a recommended role model for public speaking.
- Do not fidget. It is bad to jingle change in your pocket or repeatedly run your fingers through your hair, or do any one of a thousand other irritating things.
- Do not use any single gesture to excess. This applies even to good ones.

People use hand movements and gestures repeatedly in everyday conversation. Watch them and see. You will probably be surprised at the extent of their use. They are natural, fluid movements, and are usually relatively restrained. You normally do not notice them because they are so natural. It is fluid natural movements and gestures that you should adopt when speaking.

This does not mean that you should not use more emphatic gestures at times, particularly to emphasise key points. Most good speakers do this. To take just one example, President Kennedy had an effective way of bringing his right hand up and down when stressing something important.

As a useful rule of thumb, the bigger the hall and audience the more dramatic should be the gestures. An intimate shrug will be lost on a person sitting fifty yards away. At its most extreme this is illustrated by Adolph Hitler speaking at a Nuremberg Rally. The message was objectionable, but the delivery was effective on the day.

The speaking position

There are few things more difficult than speaking from the centre of a group. It does not usually happen to principal speakers who normally speak from a top table, or from a prepared position. But it frequently does happen to a person performing such tasks as proposing a vote of thanks. The unfortunate speaker must always have his back to part of the group. Gyrating round whilst speaking is not a good response to the problem.

Fortunately there is an ideal solution, though one that is taken by surprisingly few people. **Do not do it**. Just take a few steps to the edge of the group and speak from there. The answer is as simple as that.

Time

The importance of preparing a speech to a pre-set target time has already been mentioned. You should not lose sight of the time whilst you are speaking. This advice is intended to be taken literally – you should not lose sight of the time whilst you are speaking.

It is bad idea to glance at a watch on your wrist. It is almost impossible to hide the gesture and it may distract the audience. At worst it may get them wondering why you have not yet finished. It is much better to put a small timer, or your watch, within your line of vision but out of sight of the audience (e.g. flat on the table or under the lectern).

Last minute insertions

No matter how well your speech has been prepared, it may be possible to improve upon it by a last minute topical addition or alteration. It is of course also possible to have a bad effect, but you should look for opportunities to make a topical alteration, such as:

- in order to reply to a previous speaker
- to add right up-to-date information. Perhaps you are fundraising and the total sum raised to date has become known, or a particularly large pledge has just been made
- in order to take advantage of something said to you whilst you are waiting to speak. Perhaps you can include a personal reference to someone present.

Audiences like to hear something topical and which shows that the speaker is not rigidly bound by a prepared text.

SUMMARY
1 Make any necessary equipment checks in advance.
2 Dress appropriately and present yourself well.
3 Act as though you are meant to be there.
4 Make sure that you are heard.
5 Try and achieve vocal variety.
6 Nurture audience reaction.
7 Look at individuals for a few seconds at a time. Include all sections of the audience.
8 Aim for natural gestures. Do not fidget.
9 Change your speaking position if necessary.
10 Watch the time as you speak.
11 If there is a good opportunity to include something spontaneous or topical, take it.

7

THE USE OF
MICROPHONES AND
VISUAL AIDS

Microphones and visual aids are all intended to make your presentation more effective. Microphones enable you to be heard, or heard more easily. Props and visual aids should enhance the effectiveness of your performance. If misused, microphones and visual aids can at best be ineffective, and at worst cause havoc. This chapter is intended to help you ensure that problems are avoided and that the intended benefits are achieved.

The use of microphones

Most inexperienced speakers approach their first use of a microphone with apprehension. This is wise because it can lead to all sorts of problems. You will probably have seen speakers crouched in a rigid position, mesmerised by a microphone and not able to achieve effective contact with the audience. Furthermore, you will probably have seen audiences driven to distraction by exasperating hums and whistles.

The first question to ask is if the use of a microphone is really necessary. Many speakers use one when they could well manage without. Good speakers can speak to quite large groups without electronic assistance, and of course it was not available to many great speakers in the past. Gladstone's Midlothian Campaign consisted of numerous long speeches, a lot delivered in the open air, and usually to very large crowds. On many occasions the audiences numbered several thousands, and he did it all before the invention of the microphone.

It is well worth seeking an opportunity to practise before the actual event. More than that, it is a good idea to take any opportunity to practise. You never know when the experience will prove useful. If you are on good terms with the organisers you could arrive half an hour early at some event and just have a go. It is certainly advisable to try and practise with the actual microphone on the day of your speech, and before the audience arrives.

The ideal situation is one where the presence of a microphone is not noticed by the listeners. You in turn should almost, but not quite, forget that it is there. If the microphone is in a fixed position you can only move a certain distance away from it. If you go too far your voice will fade. Apart from this restriction you should speak as though it was not there.

A clip-on radio microphone has several advantages. It is a small device that can be clipped to a dress or suit, and once in place it does not inhibit movement. Once it is safely installed and adjusted you should be able to disregard it.

Before leaving the subject of microphones, there are two traps that should be pointed out:

- A microphone may pick up remarks not intended for broadcasting, so make sure that it is switched off when not in use. It is a good idea to check this before muttering to a neighbour your frank views about the chairman's dress sense or weight problem.
- A microphone is designed to avoid the need for shouting. If you nevertheless still shout, a very loud noise indeed may result.

Visual aids

It is your choice whether or not you use visual aids. Many good speakers do not use them at all, or use them only rarely. Visual aids are usually unsuitable for very short speeches and for such speeches as a toast at a wedding. A really apt visual aid, well prepared and well presented, can be the highlight of a speech. It can make the speech memorable and be the key factor in getting across a message.

Visual aids can spoil a speech if they are inappropriate or badly presented. This is most unlikely to happen if you study the following hints and act on the advice:

- Visual aids should be central to the message of the speech and should enhance the understanding of it. They should not be put in just for effect and have little connection with what is said.
- You should always deliver your speech to the audience, and not let the visual aids distract you from this. Do not turn your back on the audience and talk to a screen. Do not look down more than is absolutely necessary to look at an overhead projector. Do not fiddle with the equipment or aid whilst you talk.
- Visual aids should be big enough to be readily seen by the whole audience. This is a very common failing indeed. Visual aids are almost never too big, and frequently are too small. Take heed of the mistake of a fly fisherman giving a talk on his hobby to a group of seventy people. He brought with him a box of his favourite fishing flies, and throughout his talk he held up the appropriate fly between a finger and thumb. The flies were fascinating but were so tiny that even people a few feet away could not see them. He learned by the experience and when he repeated the talk on a different occasion he held up the box at the beginning, and invited the audience to have a close look when he had finished.
- Visual aids should be simple and uncluttered. This is especially true if they are in the form of words or figures. There should only be a very few words or figures. This is all that an audience can take in, even if they can see them properly. For example it is no good giving a mass of figures on truancy from schools. An audience can only assimilate something like the following:

1992	12%
1993	13%
1994	14%
1995	16%

- Check the equipment and visual aids yourself shortly before use. For the sake of your own peace of mind, to say nothing of family relationships and friendships, it is better to do it yourself. Make sure that everything is present and in the right order. Make sure that everything works. It can, for example, wreck a presentation if some of the slides are upside down or in the wrong order.

- Graphics can be a very useful aid to understanding and much better than figures. You might like to consider graphs, bar charts, and so on. For example, the truancy figures given earlier could well be shown in the form of a graph or a bar chart. This would graphically illustrate that the figures are rising and that the problem is getting worse.

Different types of visual aids

There are numerous types of visual aids. The following are the main ones together with advice on how to use them most effectively.

Handouts

These are very simple, very effective, and in appropriate cases highly recommended. A handout is a mass of information that a listener can take away and study after the presentation. Of course, some may take it away but not study it.

Handouts can vary from a single piece of paper up to dozens of sheets. They stand a better chance of being studied if they are well written and well spaced out.

The golden rule for a speaker is that a handout should be distributed at the end, not at the beginning. If they are given out in advance, some members of the audience will study the handout rather than listen to the speaker. The audience should be told at the start that a handout will be available later. This may prevent the listeners needing to take notes and will enable them to give full attention to the presentation. It enables the speaker to concentrate on broad principles, with the detail to follow in the handout.

35mm slides

These could be home-made, but you may prefer to have them professionally produced. It may not be a cheap option. If they are well produced and appropriate they can be extremely effective. The best way of using them is by means of hand-held device linked to a carousel. It should not be necessary to black out the room but care should be taken that there is no glare on the screen. As with all visual aids, the speaker should remember to talk to the audience and not to the screen.

It is very important that the slides are inserted into the carousel in the right order, not upside down, and not back to front. You should always make a last minute check yourself. A good way of preparing is to put paper stickers on the mounting and number each slide. The numbers should be in the same spot (e.g. bottom right-hand corner) and numbered 1, 2, 3, 4, 5, etc. It should then be easy to check that they are inserted correctly into the carousel. Your notes should be clearly marked with the slide numbers and the place where each slide should appear.

A good hotel may well be able to provide the necessary equipment. If it cannot be freely obtained it may be hired relatively cheaply.

Overhead projectors

The use of an overhead projector is generally not as effective as the use of 35mm slides. However, it does have two advantages:

- the slides are much cheaper
- it is possible to write on the slides during the course of the presentation.

Slides may be completed before use. Alternatively, they can be used as a skeleton and completed during the talk by writing on the acetate. This may be particularly appropriate for an educational talk where questions can be listed in advance and the answers written in during the presentation.

A few minutes' practice is highly recommended, and care should be taken not to disregard the audience whilst writing or changing the slides.

Flip charts

These are cheap and relatively effective when speaking to small groups. For the best results:

- write thickly
- keep it simple
- do not put too much detail on each sheet
- use large, bold letters and graphics.

SUMMARY

1 Consider if the use of a microphone is really necessary.
2 Practise with a microphone in advance. Take different opportunities but especially practise with the microphone to be used.
3 When the microphone has been properly set up, disregard it as much as possible.
4 Do not shout near the microphone and do not move too far away from it.
5 Always speak to the audience, not to a visual aid.
6 Do a last minute check of visual aids. This is especially important if you are using slides.
7 Visual aids should be relatively simple, and big enough to be seen.
8 Do not include too much detail on a slide or flip chart.

8

SPEECHES AT FAMILY OCCASIONS

Speeches at wedding receptions deserve, and get, a chapter all to themselves. This chapter covers the other family milestones, all of which should be happy events. They include:

- wedding anniversaries
- christenings
- birthdays
- engagements.

The latter part of this chapter includes specimen speeches for the different events, but in all cases the following general guidelines should be kept in mind.

The speeches will normally be given by a family member or by an old family friend. There is usually no set length and the speaker is free to speak for as long as he thinks is appropriate. Care should be taken that the speech does not go on for too long as can easily happen at family occasions. Perhaps it is because the speaker knows everyone so well and has a large store of anecdotes. Take care not to yield to this temptation, and keep a firm eye on time.

The speaker's tone should be wholly positive and he should praise the principal participants. This praise should go to the limits of what can sincerely be said, but not beyond those limits. People will appreciate sincere compliments, both to themselves and others. But compliments known not to be well deserved may not be received in this manner. Maybe Uncle Henry gets up at noon and leaves Aunt Ethel to do all the work. If so, do not praise him for his hard work. Say nothing on this subject and praise some of his other qualities. Perhaps he is a very kind man who is much loved by his grandchildren.

Most family groupings have the possibility of discord, and the speaker should keep in mind any potential disharmony. You should consider if any topics should not be included and if any particular person absolutely must be mentioned by name.

Family occasions lend themselves to nostalgia and the telling of anecdotes about the family past. This is excellent, but make sure that they are not embarrassing to anyone present. Only positive recollections should be included. It is a time for family heroes not family villains.

There is usually scope for emotion. Most people can remember a family occasion when someone spoke in a really moving way.

Humour is usually highly appropriate and appreciated. As with anecdotes, humour should not be embarrassing to anyone present. It should of course be really funny, and preferably not too prolonged.

———— Specimen speeches ————

Specimen toast to mark a silver wedding anniversary

- **TIME** *3–4 minutes*

  ❢ We meet here tonight to honour two exceptional people, Jim and Karen. They are exceptional in several ways, notably the work that they do together at the youth club. Then there is Jim's model engineering and Karen's bee keeping.

  But more than exceptional people, they are an exceptional couple. They have achieved together what most couples fail to achieve. I am afraid that it is true. About a third of marriages end in divorce, and in some sad cases one of the partners dies in the first twenty-five years. And we all know that many marriages survive with the partners no longer the happy couple that set out on the adventure together.

Taken together, this adds up to more than half. So a couple staying together for twenty-five years, enjoying all the years along the way, and still in love at the end of it, are the exception.

Jim and Karen are such a couple. Like some of you, I was at their wedding twenty-five years ago, and I saw them set out together on that journey. Tonight is a major milestone and there are more milestones to come. I for one have every intention of being there in twenty-five years' time when they celebrate their golden wedding.

Life is never easy and it has not been downhill all the way for them. But they coped. They coped last year when Jim lost his job and we are all delighted that he found another one so quickly. Then there was the disaster of the fire, but again they coped.

No speech like this would be complete without mentioning the two children and it is wonderful to see Peter and Roger here tonight. I realise that I should not call them children, especially as they are both doing so well in their careers, and especially as they are both now over eight feet tall. It really is marvellous that they have both come so far to be here tonight.

So, ladies and gentlemen, it is time to salute an exceptional couple. Please be upstanding. The toast is to Jim and Karen. ❥

This speech is most definitely only suitable if the speaker knows that the couple are happily married. If this is not the case it would not be appropriate and some other approach should be used.

The speech has humour in just one place, the reference to the height of the two boys.

This may be considered as an all-purpose work horse of a speech. It can be readily adapted as follows, in order to meet different individual requirements:

- The opening praises their achievements. You can substitute different achievements.
- It refers to difficult times. Every marriage has difficult times and you can substitute different details.
- You can substitute different family details and different humour.
- The ending is suitable for all occasions.

Specimen toast to mark a silver wedding anniversary

- **TIME** *3–4 minutes*

❝ This being a silver wedding anniversary I would like to tell you a story about a couple celebrating their twenty-fifth anniversary. They were a happily married couple and they did not keep secrets from each other. But there was just one exception. The wife kept a safe in the bedroom and the husband did not know what was in it.

Then on their twenty-fifth wedding anniversary he found the key and opened the safe. He was puzzled to find two chicken eggs and £1,000. He had to know, so when she came home he told her what he had found and asked her why there were two eggs in the safe.

She looked rather sad and told him that each time she had been unfaithful to him she had put an egg in the safe. As you can imagine the man was a little upset but he loved his wife and, after all, twice in twenty-five years is not so very bad. So he forgave her.

This just left the question of where the £1,000 had come from and he asked her that too. 'Oh', she replied, 'Every time I got a dozen eggs I sold them and put the money in the safe!'

Ladies and gentlemen it is my privilege to propose the toast to Colin and Margaret. Like the couple in the story they are happily married, but the similarity ends there.

Some of us know them as valued members of the family. Others know them as very good friends. Some, like myself, were privileged to be present at their wedding twenty-five years ago. The rest of us have come to know them over the years.

No matter, we all congratulate them on reaching this milestone, and we all wish them every success in the many years to come. And needless to say we thank them for their hospitality tonight.

Ladies and gentlemen! The toast is Colin and Margaret. ❞

The main part of the speech is the funny story. It is relatively long which is a disadvantage, but it sounds intriguing during the telling and will almost certainly retain the interest of the audience. The punch line is a surprise and is extremely funny. It cannot really be said to be smutty and should not cause offence. The only circumstance in which it would not be appropriate would be if the speaker suspected unfaithfulness on the part of one of the partners. A funny story, this one or some other one, is an effective introduction to the rest of the toast. This toast is relatively short but the story could lay the foundation for a much longer recital.

Specimen speech for a golden wedding anniversary, May 1996

- **TIME** *$2^1/_2$–$3^1/_2$ minutes*

  ❦ A lot of important things happened in May 1946.

  Prime Minister Attlee announced his plan to give independence to India.

  Bread was put on ration for the first time ever.

  Winston Churchill predicted that Britain and the United States would give common citizenship. Hmm! We are still waiting on that one.

  And money went so much further then. You could buy a two-door Morris car for £290. Mind you, George only earned £4 a week so he could not buy one.

  But by far the most important event was the wedding of George and Mary. It was a happy wedding and a marriage that lasted, and here we are celebrating that event.

  Since that wedding in Amersham Church, George and Mary have lived fifty happy years together. They have produced three children, all here tonight, Sally, Michael and Sandra. And they have been blessed with seven grandchildren.

  They have founded the family business together, and worked in it right up to last year.

  And they are so well regarded in this town. George has been churchwarden for twenty years and Mary practically runs the Women's Institute. And there are all the things that they do together.

There is a lot to celebrate and the story has more episodes to run yet. Before I leave this hotel I am going to book this room for 16th May, 2006. That's for the diamond wedding party and you are all invited. So keep the date free.

George and Mary it is wonderful to share this moment with you. This present is with affection from us all, your family and your friends. We hope that you like it and thank you for this evening. **9**

A golden wedding anniversary is an appropriate time to look back on events fifty years ago. The same technique can of course be used for ruby wedding anniversaries and to mark many other events.

A wedding in May 1946 has been assumed but it can be done for any month, or even day if preferred. The information can be obtained at most libraries from such books as *Chronicle of the 20th Century*, which records events day by day.

The anniversary details are a good introduction to the personal parts that follow. These can be long or short. As with the silver wedding speeches, individual details can be substituted for the personal details given in the specimen.

Specimen toast at a christening party

● **TIME** *3–3¹/₂ minutes*

6 A speech at a christening is, almost by definition, a happy speech. A christening is a time for happiness and it is a time for optimism. We all know that young Robert will have his problems over the years, everybody does. But it is impossible not to believe that he will overcome them, and that he is going to have a long, happy, healthy and successful life.

Why do I say this? I say it first of all because I just feel that it is true. When you look at the baby you just cannot feel anything else. But also, look at the advantages that he has.

For a start he is English and has therefore drawn first prize in the lottery of life. Not just British, but English. And even more than that he is a Lancastrian. He will grow up in God's own county, and when in Lancashire will have the privilege of raising his glass to the toast 'The Queen – The Duke of Lancaster'.

Furthermore, Robert has the very real advantage of starting life as a member of the Lofthouse family. He has two wonderful parents, three wonderful grandparents, and a whole host of sisters-cousins-and-aunts. To say nothing of family friends, so many of whom are here today.

And he is going to have the support of four upright Godparents. With all that going for him, how could he possibly fail?

Before proposing Robert's health I am of course going to thank Bill and Susan for today's hospitality, especially as they did the catering themselves. We have all enjoyed ourselves and it went without a hitch.

Now – the toast. Ladies and gentlemen. Please be upstanding. It is my pleasure and privilege to propose the toast to the newly christened Robert. To Robert. ❾

A christening is a time for happiness, optimism and praise. It is not the time for doubts, criticism or negative thoughts. This of course said with the proviso that the baby is healthy. The toast would need redrafting if this was not the case.

It is normal for the toast to be given either by one of the Godparents, or by an old family friend. The above toast is intended to be given by the latter, in which case it is normal to give a favourable mention to all the Godparents as well as the parents.

Light-hearted and self-satisfied praise for a county or region is likely to be well received almost anywhere. Curiously, the greater the distance from the capital the greater is likely to be the regional pride. The use of this technique need not be restricted to England. American readers might refer to Bergen County, New Jersey, for example, and an Australian advises that a suitable reference to an Australian state would receive an enthusiastic response.

As readers may know, the Duke of Lancaster is one of the Monarch's titles and it is the traditional loyal toast if made in Lancashire. The reference to sisters, cousins, and aunts comes from *HMS Pinafore* by Gilbert and Sullivan.

Specimen toast at a birthday party

● **TIME** *4–5 minutes*

❻ Politicians are fond of saying that 'what you see is what you get'. It quite often leads to disappointment because you do not always quite get what you think you have seen. And you sometimes get one or two unwelcome things that you have not seen at all.

If Paul were to say 'what you see is what you get' it would be quite true. That's because he is a straightforward sort of guy, and all the admirable qualities that we see really are there.

But 'what you see is what you get' would be less than the whole truth. For a start you have to check his age with a calendar. You see a man just turned forty, but in reality he is fifty today. It is uncanny and it makes me think of Oscar Wilde's *A Picture of Dorian Gray*. I reckon he must keep a picture up in the attic.

More seriously, you get more than you see because Paul is such a modest man, and he does a lot for people without making a song and dance about it. Last year when Julie was in hospital he practically ran a taxi service taking all the family over to see her. I for one could not have got there every day without his help. Numerous people could tell stories about Paul's kindness and of how he doesn't take the credit that he could.

You may have gathered that I am an admirer of Paul. You would be quite right. I am. That is one of the reasons why I am making this speech tonight.

The other reason is that I have known him for such a long time. We shared babysitters and I pinched his sandwiches when we went on the cubs' outing. We were eight at the time. I was also at his twenty-first birthday party and I was best man at his wedding to Trudy.

Which brings me to the family, Paul and Trudy – the names go together like Laurel and Hardy or Torvill and Dean. Say one and you think of the other. Like Manchester United and championship or Tottenham Hotspur and relegation. And there are Ben and David as well. I do not know a happier family.

And it's that happy family that we have to thank for the party tonight. There was an awful lot of work and it did not just happen. Trudy in particular has worked all week producing this buffet. But back to Paul. The birthday boy. Fifty years young today. On behalf of all your family and friends I congratulate you on everything that you have achieved and I look forward to what is still to come. Now ladies and gentlemen please be upstanding. The toast is Paul. **9**

It is unfortunate if politicians read this section, but the opening remarks are likely to be popular. This is because nearly everyone will agree with the remarks, though perhaps with different politicians in mind. It is relevant because it is a link with Paul's characteristics. The speech is of course only suitable if the subject does have the admirable qualities mentioned. Real deeds, events and names should be substituted.

Humour about football teams is usually popular, especially if known keen supporters are present. Perhaps the speaker's favourite team can be inserted in place of Manchester United, and the subject's favourite team can be inserted in place of Tottenham Hotspur. Other sports or teams could be mentioned, for example basketball or baseball, if appropriate.

In *A Picture of Dorian Gray*, Oscar Wilde has a portrait ageing in the attic whilst the owner stays youthful. A reference to this is a nice way of complementing a person beyond a certain age who has kept a youthful appearance. Of course, it is only appropriate if the person really does look youthful.

Specimen speech at an engagement party

- **TIME** *2–2¹/₂ minutes*

  ❝ Pretty! More than that – good looking! A lovely smile.

  That gorgeous hair that everyone admires.

  And all the housekeeping skills – a marvellous cook.

  And that's just Peter! Wait till I tell you about Lynda! Seriously though, I am here to propose the toast to a marvellous couple. Between them they have all the qualities that I have just mentioned. I will not say which person has each quality, except to say that I was thinking more of Lynda when I used the word pretty. Peter is pretty good at football though.

  I have known Lynda for a long time. In fact, I have known her so long that I was at her christening. I remember her first day at school. She told me that she quite liked it but that she did not think that she would go again. But she did. And she did so well that she finished her education with a good degree.

Later I watched her career blossom. And I watched a marvellous girl turn into a marvellous adult.

I must admit that I have a prejudice against Peter. That is because he is going to take Lynda away from us. But apart from that there is an awful lot to like about him.

They are in short a well-matched couple who deserve every happiness together. Congratulations to you both.

Ladies and gentlemen. The toast is to the engagement – Lynda and Peter. **❾**

The humour in this can be used in any speech praising the qualities of a man and a woman. The trick is to praise either obviously male or obviously female qualities, and then indicate that you had the other partner in mind. It is best followed up with genuine and uncomplicated praise.

SUMMARY

1 Do not go on for too long.
2 Only include praise and positive thoughts.
3 Think if any topics should be avoided. Do not embarrass anyone.
4 Praise should go to the limits of sincerity, but not beyond.
5 Emotion may have a valuable place in the speech.
6 Nostalgia and family anecdotes may be appropriate.
7 Humour will be welcomed.

9

TOASTS AT A WEDDING RECEPTION

This chapter may well be the most studied in the whole book, at least by the male readers. This is because most men get married at least once and many men perform the duties of the best man at least once. In later life many men can expect to be father of a bride. The modern trend towards increasing divorce, and remarriage, means that many wedding receptions and wedding speeches take place. There were 311,564 weddings in Britain in the latest year for which full records are available. There were also 160,400 divorces.

For quite a few men, a wedding speech is the only one that they will ever give in public. For quite a few more, a wedding speech is the first one that they will give in public. Most wedding reception audiences will be very tolerant and willing the speaker to do well.

—— The usual wedding speeches ——

The principal participants can agree to have whatever speeches they wish. This may be a dozen toasts down to nothing at all, and you may encounter a different format to the one described here. A different format is more likely if the wedding is a second or subsequent one, or if the couple come from a minority religion or culture. This book does not tell anyone what speeches they should have at their wedding reception. However, the majority still choose the following traditional three speeches:

1 The bride's father proposes the toast to the bride and groom. It usually is the bride's father, but it may be one of the bride's other

relatives, or an old family friend. This will be the case if the bride's father is dead, cannot be present, or for some reason (usually fright) is not willing to do it.

2 The bridegroom replies to the toast, and concludes by proposing the toast to the bridesmaids or matron of honour.

3 The best man replies on behalf of the bridesmaids or matron of honour.

The role of the women

The march of feminism has eroded many traditions, but curiously it is still usual for all wedding speeches to be given by men. The bridegroom speaks for his wife, and the best man speaks for the bridesmaids or the matron of honour. Female readers may be enraged or relieved at this, quite probably both. But to repeat a point made earlier, the participants are free to organise the speeches as they wish.

Although still unusual, it is becoming more common for the bride to say a few words. If this does happen her speech is normally very short, and is given either at the end of the speeches or, more usually, directly after her husband's speech.

The importance of time

It is well worth the speakers discussing this in advance, amongst themselves and with the other key people. As with other matters, there are no absolute rules. You are free to do what you want and what you think the other people will want. However, it sometimes happens that wedding speeches are too long, and you may well recall wedding receptions when this has happened. For some reason it is often the bride's father who is the main offender.

Do consider how much time is available. At some receptions the room has to be vacated at a certain time. Do also consider the likely wishes of the guests.

It may well be that a total of about fifteen minutes is a good target. Allowing for the toasts, and the sitting and standing, this means that each of the three speakers has an average of around four minutes.

Positive points that you should remember

- Try and enjoy your speech. Many do, at least in retrospect. A wedding reception is expensive and normally a very happy occasion. The speakers are usually known and liked by most of the audience, and will probably have the active encouragement of most of them. These are all good reasons to enjoy giving the speech. Apart from anything else you are more likely to do well if you are enjoying it.
- Two of the three traditional speeches end by proposing a toast. If you are making these speeches remember to actually say the words of the toast at the end, and remember to fill your glass before you speak. If you are one of the people being toasted you should stay seated whilst the others stand and toast you.
- Give careful thought to the length of the speech, and then keep to your plan.
- A wedding is an emotional time. It is all right to use emotion in your speech.
- The audience will appreciate humour.
- The audience will appreciate sincerity, especially sincerely expressed thank yous.
- Consider carefully who should be thanked by name and who should be mentioned by name.
- One or two good anecdotes will almost certainly be appreciated. They should be good and there will probably only be time for one or two.
- A wedding is, or should be, an entirely happy event. This should be reflected in the speeches which should be entirely happy and positive. This does not mean that a reference could not be made to a dead relative, and the remark made that it is sad that this fine person cannot be present.

— Mistakes that should be avoided —

- Do not speak for too long. Neither should your speech be too short, but too long is more common.

- Do not tell jokes that are smutty or in bad taste. Remember that the audience will probably be mixed age and mixed sex. It may contain people who are easily offended.
- Do not say anything that will embarrass anyone, and do not refer to any previous marriages or partners. You may have seen the film *Four Weddings and a Funeral* in which the best man makes a speech with uproarious references to previous girlfriends. It is marvellous entertainment but should not be repeated in real life.
- Do not say anything negative and avoid reference to any family disputes.

— The toast to the bride and groom —

The main point of this toast is to say nice, sincere things about the bride and groom. It is best to do this individually and then in combination as a couple. The following is a straightforward, relatively short example of a typical toast, to be delivered by the father of the bride.

Specimen toast to the bride and groom

- **TIME** *2¹/₂–3 minutes*

    ❛ It is my privilege to propose the toast to the bride and groom. And seldom can a duty have been such a pleasure.

    It is a pleasure, first of all, because it is such a happy day. Eighty people gathered for the purpose of honouring Michael and Caroline.

    And especially it is a pleasure because it is Michael and Caroline. All brides are radiant on their wedding day. And Caroline is more radiant than most. And all bridegrooms are splendid fellows. This is certainly true of Michael. I know because he told me so himself.

    I will admit to a little bias when I describe Caroline's qualities. After all, I have known her for a long time, longer than anyone else apart from her mother. And Rosemary joins me in telling you of our pride in our daughter. We have watched with satisfaction as she developed into the young woman who you see today.

We are proud of so many things. Her childhood, her achievements at school, and of course her degree. We are proud of her career and of the new position that she successfully gained last month. We are proud of her practical and home-making abilities, and best of all her wonderful personality. Are these things inherited? I look at her mother and think that perhaps they are.

Michael too brings great qualities to the marriage. Obviously, I speak with less authority, but it is clearly true. A man who scores twenty-four goals in one season, and sings in the church choir as well, has a great deal to recommend him.

So we have an exceptional bride, an exceptional groom, and more than that an exceptional couple. Would you please rise and join me in the toast to the bride and groom. **9**

The above toast contains humour in just one place. You may like to make the speech more humorous, but on no account lose sight of the main point. This is to pay tribute to the bride and groom. You might like to include an anecdote, but do ensure that it is not unduly embarrassing.

It may be appropriate to be a little more emotional. In particular you may want to refer to people who sadly cannot be present.

The following speech is designed to be given by an uncle due to the sad absence of the bride's father. It contains an anecdote and a little more humour.

Specimen toast to the bride and groom

- **TIME** *About 2 minutes*

6 I am very honoured to propose the toast to John and Mary. Much as I have to say, and much as I am enjoying myself, I just wish that it could be Mary's father standing here now. He contributed so much and he would have been so proud of Mary. He would have done a good job with the toast too.

But we know that it cannot be. So you've got Uncle Jim instead.

I am going to start by telling John what he already knows. He is marrying into a jolly good family. Apart from everything else they are all good cooks. And it's hereditary. Mary is as well. And there is more. If John and Mary ever start a business they will be quite a team. I knew that Mary had a sharp business brain when she was only seven years old. She sold me a bunch of daffodils to give to my wife on Easter Sunday. They were only twenty pence. I found out later that she had picked them from my window box whilst I was out of the room.

John. Welcome to our family. And I know that Mary appreciates the welcome that she is getting to yours. It is marvellous that you all managed to come today.

Ladies and gentlemen, we have a radiant bride, we have a charming and handsome groom. Please join me in the toast to the bride and groom, John and Mary. 9

The bridegroom's reply

The main part of the bridegroom's reply is usually a list of thank yous. He should think of how many of the following it is appropriate to include:

- thank you to the proposer of the toast, for the things said
- a general thank you to the bride's parents and a tribute to the bride
- a thank you to his own parents
- a general thank you to the guests, for coming and also for their presents
- thank you to the best man
- thank you to anyone who has made a special contribution such as making dresses, making a cake, driving a car, or accommodating guests
- thank you to the bridesmaids.

The speech concludes with a toast to the bridesmaids.

Of course the speech should be lightened to prevent it appearing to be just a list. This may be done with one or two anecdotes or humorous touches. The use of the phrase 'My wife and I' nearly always causes laughter, especially if accompanied by a knowing look and a pause.

The following are two all-purpose replies:

Specimen reply by the bridegroom

* **TIME** *3–4 minutes*

    ❝ (Pause before standing up.)

    Please excuse the pause. It's just that I was not sure who Bill was talking about. I thought for a moment that I had strayed into the wrong wedding reception.

    There were all those lovely things about Jill, and then he was talking about some young man. What was it he said? Hard working, successful, friendly, nice personality. It took some time before I realised that he meant me.

    Now that it has sunk in I would like to respond with a big thank you. First of all to Bill for the toast and the nice things that he said about Jill and myself. And more generally, to both Bill and Joan, for doing such a wonderful job for twenty-one years. And then for making welcome the man who was lucky enough to marry their daughter.

    And I want to thank my parents as well. For all that they have done for me, and for the way that they helped Jill and me in the lead-up to today.

    My wife and I (pause) are delighted to see you all, particularly as some of you have come a very long way. We have been over-whelmed by the lovely presents and thank you all for them.

    Down there is a lady who deserves a special mention, Aunty Connie who made the wedding cake. We are looking forward to cutting it in a few minutes time. You have all seen how beautifully it is decorated and as a paid-up member of the Aunty Connie cake club I can tell you that it will taste gorgeous as well.

    I think that you will agree that not much has gone wrong so far, which brings me to Paul my best man. I am grateful for his support and all that he has done. I have heard of a best man bringing two rings, in case one got lost. But have you ever heard of one bringing three?

Now finally, and very importantly, the bridesmaids. It is my pleasure to thank them for their help to Jill. It is an emotional day and they helped Jill be at her best, and were so beautiful and charming as well.

I now propose the toast to the bridesmaids, Laura and Jo. Please be upstanding. To the bridesmaids. 〝

Specimen reply by the bridegroom

● **TIME** *2¹/₂–3 minutes*

❝ My wife and I (pause) thank you for your good wishes and the lovely things that you have just said.

It is traditional for the bridegroom to thank the bride's parents for bringing her up successfully, and then to thank them for ending their job by giving her to him. Well! I am going to do half of that. My wife certainly does thank you for all that you have done, and judging by the results I have every reason to do the same.

But I am not going to thank you for giving her to me. Maria is an independent, successful young woman, who cannot be given by anybody to anybody. That is part of your success and I reckon that you did a pretty good job.

And talking of good jobs, there are others here who we would like to thank sincerely. There are my parents too.

And all of you who spent an afternoon with us on a day when Chelsea were playing at home (meaningful glance at one particular person). But, joking aside, we do thank you for coming, and for all those wonderful presents.

Which leaves Sally, Maria's matron of honour and it leaves Peter, my best man. I am grateful for the splendid support that Peter has given me. I am married, I was on time, I am sober, and I am only slightly insolvent. He did a lot, and thank you Peter.

Finally, it is my pleasure and privilege to propose the toast to Sally. Never have the duties of matron of honour been done so beautifully, and with so much charm. Ladies and gentlemen, the toast is to the matron of honour. To Sally. 〝

———— The best man's speech ————

The audience may well be particularly looking forward to the speech of the best man. He is often a popular person, and indeed this is probably one of the reasons why he has been asked to do the job. The audience will probably be looking forward to humour, anecdotes, and a general light touch.

It is up to the best man not to disappoint them. It is usual to include some humour, but unless the speaker is very assured it is best not to make the speech just a procession of jokes. It is fine to include one or two anecdotes, interesting and funny and at the expense of the bridegroom. However, care should be taken that they are not too embarrassing. Only a small amount of vulgarity should be considered.

The speech is in response to a toast to the bridesmaids, and it should therefore start by acknowledging this and thanking the groom for his compliments. The speech often includes a section reading some or all of the telegrams, and a reference to people who cannot be present. This is usually done towards the end.

The best man will usually say what is still to happen. For example he may say that the guests will be staying in the room for a further half hour and then moving to the garden. This comes at the end of the speech, but it is not a good idea to conclude with a business item such as this. It is better to conclude with a joke, or something interesting or inspiring.

If the bride is to say a few words, and if she is to speak at the end rather than after the bridegroom, the best man will conclude by introducing her.

Specimen reply by the best man

- **TIME** *$4^1/_2$–$5^1/_2$ minutes*

  ❝ It is my privilege to reply on behalf of the two bridesmaids. They would have been far too modest to say so themselves, but every word was completely true. On behalf of Catherine and Jo, thank you for saying them. It is so nice to know how much their efforts have been appreciated.

I was flattered and a little puzzled when Gary asked me to be his best man. I can only think that he wanted some frank advice from a man of experience. And it certainly is true that things do seem to happen to me.

Only last week Gary and I were sitting on a bus opposite a very beautiful young woman. She was wearing a badge saying 'N.A.N. – PRESIDENT'. Gary asked what N.A.N. meant, and she said that it was the National Association of Nymphomaniacs. It was their mission in life to find out which race made the world's best lovers.

Gary's mind was on today, so I asked her if they had reached a conclusion. Now this will surprise you! She said that it was a dead heat between the Red Indians and the Israelis.

We exchanged names so that we could talk about it later. Her name was Sophie Barton, and I told her that mine was Hiawatha Cohen.

Gary appreciated the joke, but then he would. He has got a terrific sense of humour. Laura knows that by now, but just in case she doesn't I will give her an example. When Gary was eleven his father planted a dozen rose bushes in the front garden. It was November and the rose bushes were just bare twigs. Gary went out at midnight and tied twenty plastic roses to each bush. Then when his parents pulled the curtains in the morning they looked out on a mass of flowers. They have only just got over it.

It was a happy joke, like all of them. And like everyone else I am wishing all the luck in the world to two happy people, Gary and Laura.

It is good to see so many friends here, but there are a few who just could not make it. I have been asked to pass on their best wishes, and in particular the good wishes of Joy and Bob Jenkins, Claud Murphy, and the Brown family who are still in New Zealand. All these have sent telegrams and there are others as well. Gary and Laura have asked me to leave them on the table, so do look at them later if you would like to.

'Later' starts in two minutes' time and Gary and Laura will be leaving at six. I do not know where they are going, all I know is what I saw on the luggage labels. Does anyone know which country Air France flies to?

I hope that they enjoy every minute of it and, ladies and gentlemen, please enjoy the rest of the afternoon. ❯

The bride's speech

As stated earlier, the bride does not normally speak, but it is becoming more usual. The main participants, and especially the bride, should arrange whatever speeches they wish. The bride's speech (if there is one) is usually made directly after the speech of the bridegroom, or at the end, after the speech of the best man. The bride's speech is normally short. The following is an example of what might be said:

❮ Robert has thanked everyone and I just want to add my voice to what he has said. I want to thank Robert's parents, Aunt Julia, and you all for your wonderful presents and for coming. But especially I want to thank Mum and Dad, for all they have done for me and of course for today.

They say that your wedding day is the happiest day of your life, Well! it's true. It is. ❯

SUMMARY
1 Expect to enjoy it. The audience will be on your side.
2 Do not speak for too long.
3 Do not be frightened of emotion.
4 The audience will probably hope for humour and a few very good anecdotes. Do not disappoint them.
5 It should be a happy day, so be wholly positive. Avoid reference to any family disputes.
6 Do not say anything too vulgar or in bad taste.
7 Do not embarrass anyone.

10
GENERAL AFTER DINNER TOASTS

There are literally hundreds of different toasts that you may be requested to make. In Britain it is customary to commence with the loyal toast. Among the toasts that may follow are:

- The Royal Air Force (or some other branch of the armed forces)
- The Regiment
- The School
- The Old Boys' Association or Old Girls' Association
- The Company (e.g. The Ford Motor Company at a company sponsored dinner)
- The Organisation (e.g. The Royal Society for the Prevention of Cruelty to Animals)
- The Party (e.g. The Conservative Party or in the U.S.A. The Democratic Party)
- The Mayor and Corporation (at a local civic event)
- The Association (e.g. The Law Society at a dinner of the solicitors' body)
- The Ladies
- The Guests
- Absent Friends

Toasts may be unusual or even bizarre. An example of an unusual toast is one to The Aylesbury Duck. This is proposed at an annual dinner in Aylesbury, and is in honour of the bird for which the town of Aylesbury is internationally famous. I have been given the privilege of proposing this one.

There is never a reply to the loyal toast but there is almost always a reply to other toasts.

The main part of this chapter consists of specific advice and specimen speeches for some of the more frequently encountered toasts, together with short sections on grace and the loyal toast. But first there is general advice on giving a good performance, followed by hints on mistakes to avoid.

General advice on proposing after dinner toasts

- As with all toasts you should remember to fill your own glass before rising to speak, and you should remember to conclude by actually saying the words of the toast. If you are one of the people being toasted, remember to remain seated whilst the toast is being drunk. At a large gathering you will often see people get this wrong, and embarrassed friends whispering that they should sit down. It may be that ninety-five per cent of the audience should remain seated during a toast to the guests.
- It is crucially important that you speak for the right period of time. This can mean that the speech should not be too short, but almost invariably it means that the speech should not be too long. This is probably the most common failure of after dinner speakers, and the fault most resented by audiences.
- You should think very carefully about the planned length of your speech, and if necessary take advice from the organisers or other helpful people. Planning and achieving the ideal time was covered in some detail in Chapter 2.
- In most cases the audience will be delighted by the use of humour.
- It is worth giving some thought to the likely composition of the audience. You might ask yourself if anyone should be mentioned by name, and if particular events or people deserve a section of your speech.
- You will almost always be speaking to praise people or organisations. If you are replying to a toast you will usually be speaking partly to thank someone for the honour of the toast. The general tone should therefore be one of sincere praise, perhaps even flattery.

- Be alert to the possibility of a topical addition. This advice particularly applies to a reply to a toast, where it is effective to refer to something said by the proposer.

— Mistakes that should be avoided —

- An after dinner speech is one that is always delivered after an opportunity to eat dinner, usually an opportunity to eat a lot of food and drink a lot of alcohol. Most people should only drink and eat in moderation before speaking. Some people prefer not to eat or drink at all, though this extreme step is not usually necessary.
- Do not speak for too long. This is very important.
- At all costs do not be boring. This is partly a matter of content and partly a matter of delivery. Even if your delivery is bad, make sure that you say something interesting, or better still exciting.
- Do not take advantage of the audience by pursuing personal feuds.
- Make sure that you can be heard. If necessary change your speaking position so that you are facing all the audience.

Grace

Grace is not delivered after dinner, but public speakers may be asked to say it. A few comments in this chapter are therefore appropriate.

The procedure is normally for a Chairman or President to call the group to order, and then ask for silence for Mr X who will say grace. Silence does normally follow, but if it does not Mr X should ask for silence before proceeding. It is disrespectful to say grace without the necessary attention. Sometimes waiters may unwittingly create a disturbance.

Mr X should ask everyone to rise and he then says the words of the grace. It is, of course, delivered absolutely 'straight'. The speaker should be word perfect and reading is permissible. Diction should be clear, volume reasonably loud, and the tone reverential or at least respectful.

The speaker may be given a nominated grace, or more usually is free to select one. By far the most common is the ubiquitous,

❦ For what we are about to receive, make the Lord make us truly thankful. ❧

There are hundreds of other graces and the speaker may refer to an appropriate book. He could even compose a grace. He should have regard to the occasion and the composition of the group. An example of a more overtly religious grace is:

> ❦ Be present at our table, Lord;
> Be here and everywhere adored.
> These mercies bless, and grant that we
> May feast in Paradise with Thee. ❧

This may be spoken or sung. If sung it fits well with the tune 'Remington' which is often used for the hymn *Jesus shall reign where'r the Sun.*

--------------- # The loyal toast ---------------

The loyal toast is always the first toast, and is sometimes delivered during the coffee stage of the meal. Often the Chairman will say immediately after the loyal toast 'Gentlemen you have your President's permission to smoke'. Unfortunately this statement occasionally results in laughter because some people will already be smoking. This is a pity. The Chairman may preceed the statement about smoking with 'Ladies and gentlemen' but often it is just 'Gentlemen'. This is despite the fact that women now smoke almost as much as men.

The loyal toast is always extremely short and simple. It is usually 'Ladies and gentlemen please be upstanding for the loyal toast. (pause) Her majesty the Queen'.

This toast is recognised in Britain, and in all Commonwealth countries which recognise the Queen as head of state. Other countries have a toast to their own head of state, usually naming the position rather than the person.

If more than one nationality is represented in the audience, it is hospitable to drink more than one toast, though it is not a requirement. For example at an Anglo-Irish function the toast to the Queen may be followed by a toast to the President of the Irish

Republic. If the function is in Britain the toast to the Queen would come first. If the function is in the Irish Republic the order would be reversed. Every country puts its own head of state first.

In some areas it is customary to name one of the Queen's additional titles. For example in the county of Lancashire the toast is 'The Queen – The Duke of Lancaster'.

Specimen toasts

Specimen toast to the Royal Society for the Prevention of Cruelty to Animals

- **TIME** *$3^1/_2$–$4^1/_2$ minutes*

  ❦ In many ways my task tonight is a very easy one. Why do I say that? Well, there are several reasons.

  First of all it's because everyone knows the RSPCA. It's like Save The Children and Oxfam. We all know the name and we all know the work that it does.

  And what is more everyone approves of the work. It is a good thing. Just like motherhood, the flag and apple pie. We are all in favour of it.

  And we all have the idea that the work is done well. Many of us have seen the Association's work at first hand, I certainly have, and we like what we see. Your reputation stands high.

  Of course we are a nation of animal lovers and the public will usually do what they can to help animals in distress. I saw an outstanding example during the bitter winter weather last January. I was visiting a farm and a complete herd of sixty cows were frozen solid. They were like blocks of ice.

  The farmer was in a terrible state and it looked as though they would all die. Then a marvellous thing happened. A kindly woman drove up and she said that she could help. And she did too. She sang a hymn and then she walked round and tapped each cow lightly on the nose. And instantly the ice melted, and the cows frolicked around, and ate their hay.

The farmer was overwhelmed and he wanted to give the woman a present. He got out his cheque book but she would not take anything at all. But he absolutely insisted and eventually she agreed to take £10. He asked to whom he should make the cheque payable, and she said, 'Make it payable to Thora Hird'.

Support like that helps a lot, but it is still not an easy job. Sadly, some people cause terrible suffering to animals. And of course animals need to recover from accidents and from the effects of natural causes, as well as from neglect and worse.

The work of the RSPCA will always be needed and we are fortunate that you are here to meet that need.

Mr Chairman we thank the Association for its great achievements, and we congratulate it on its present healthy state. Ladies and gentlemen. Please raise your glasses. The toast is to the RSPCA. 9

The structure of the speech is a common one for a toast to an organisation such as this. It starts with a series of compliments to the association, no doubt sincere and well merited. It then moves on to a joke, the subject of which is relevant to the toast. The joke is quite long, but it is intriguing and has a powerful punch line. If well told it should get a very good audience response. The speaker then returns to a serious note and concludes with the toast.

The joke will be well understood in Britain but other readers may appreciate an explanation. It is a pun based on the name of Thora Hird (Thaw a Herd). Thora Hird is a rather saintly actress who presents a well-known Sunday religious television programme.

The next specimen speech is a reply to the toast to the RSPCA. The responder will usually have the problem of preparing a reply without knowledge of what will be said by the proposer. However, it is very likely that compliments will have been paid to the work of the Association. It is therefore safe to prepare a reply which thanks the speaker for the kind words said.

The responder will probably want to give certain facts and figures about the Association. He or she should listen very carefully to the toast and look for an opportunity to make a topical reference to something said, and the specimen reply assumes that this has been achieved. It is usually possible to do this, though of course it is harder to do it on the night than it is to include it in a book.

Specimen reply to the toast to the Royal Society for the Prevention of Cruelty to Animals

- **TIME** *2¹/₂–3 minutes*

❝ On behalf of the RSPCA and its officers, I would like to thank you for the toast and for the compliments. We all know the work that we do, but it is very reassuring to hear that it is so well understood and so well regarded.

I was not aware of Thora Hird's work in the welfare of farm animals, but it is much appreciated and backs up our own achievements. Our own Inspectors do much in this field, and perhaps you read last week of the terrible suffering of the animals on that farm in Wiltshire. It was an RSPCA inspector who spotted what was happening, and it was our work which led to the prosecution. It was not in the papers but we managed to save nearly all the animals as well.

It was reassuring to know that our work is so well understood because some people think that we just deal with domestic animals. Nothing could be further from the truth. In fact our northern branch was able to help a baby gorilla just recently. The poor creature had been born without any knees and it was forced to move about with totally stiff legs.

But the animal had heard of our clinic and it saved up its money until it had a whole penny. And then it came to us and asked if we could give it two ape knees for a penny. Of course we did it for nothing.

I must of course end on a more serious note. Last year we found homes for 80,000 animals and we completed 218,000 treatments. Sadly, but of necessity, we undertook 67,000 humane destructions.

We are proud of our record. On behalf of our 201 branches, and on behalf of our half million members, I thank you for the toast. ❞

The joke is of course extremely corny which, if it is told with panache, is part of the attraction. However, it could be omitted, or any one of a thousand different jokes substituted.

The toast to the guests

It is usual to mention by name one or two (or three or four) of the more prominent guests. This should include the guest who will reply to the toast. It is a good idea to say something about these people's activities and the reason for their prominence, especially in relation to the particular event. Also the toast should welcome all the guests, either en bloc or in groups. Particular care should be taken with titles and positions.

As well as all this the toast should be a good speech in the ways mentioned at the start of this chapter. As with all toasts, it should not be too long and humour is likely to be appreciated.

Each event is unique and it is therefore difficult to include a typical toast to the guests. However, the following toast and response illustrate possible approaches. Assumptions have been made about the identity of the guests and also about the event.

Specimen toast to the guests

- **TIME** *3¹/₂–4¹/₂ minutes*

    ❛ It is a great pleasure for the Association to welcome so many distinguished guests to our annual dinner. We know that you lead very busy lives and we really appreciate you being here tonight.

    You are all most welcome, but in particular I would like to mention Dawn Craker, the President of the Chamber of Commerce. She is here with no fewer than twenty Chamber members. We have always had a very good relationship with the Chamber of Commerce, and tonight is going to cement it further. The return fixture is on April 8th and we look forward to joining them for the Chamber's Anniversary Dinner.

    Chamber members know that there is not much money about at the moment, but even so our local newspaper was surprised by a woman who called this morning to place an advertisement. Her husband had died and she was putting a notice in the deaths column. Insertions are at the rate of £1 a word and her notice just consisted of the two words 'Jack's Dead'.

But sadly this could not be inserted because there is a minimum charge of £5. After a lot of thought she decided to go ahead but changed the words to 'Jack's Dead – Volvo For Sale'.

I also want to welcome our Guest of Honour, Eric Pickles, and his wife Stephanie. We are looking forward to Eric's speech in a few minutes.

Eric is very well known as a leading solicitor in Norwich, and also as Chairman of the East Anglia Tourist Authority. Stephanie's crime novels are eagerly anticipated and I am told that the next one is with the publisher now.

I do not know whether or not Eric would have told us that he is a Yorkshireman, and very proud of it. But I am reminded of a comment by Roy Hattersley. He said that you should never ask a man if he is a Yorkshireman. If he is he will tell you. And if he is not, then why humiliate him.

Ladies and gentlemen. We welcome Eric and Stephanie Pickles, all the Chamber members and all our other guests. Association members will you please be upstanding and drink the toast to our guests. 9

Specimen reply to toast to the guests

- **TIME** *3–4 minutes*

  6 Mr Chairman, Sir Robert, ladies and gentlemen.

Of course I was going to tell you that I came from Yorkshire. Because what Britain needs is a bit more good old-fashioned Yorkshire grit. The Association has it, and so has our Chamber of Commerce. I just wish that a few more people had the same attitude.

Sir Robert, you are a cricketer as well as a businessman. So you will appreciate all those Yorkshire players with that gritty approach to the game. Herbert Sutcliffe, Len Hutton, Fred Truman and all the others. I just wish they were playing now.

Do you remember the 1952 Test Match against India at Headingly? No, of course not. It was before my time too. But it was Fred Truman's finest match. India were 0 for 4 and Fred had taken all four wickets. Only Polly Umrigar could stay there and he kept slowing things down by asking for the sightscreen to be moved.

They moved it twice, but when he asked a third time the umpire asked 'Just where would you like the sightscreen put Mr Umrigar?' He replied 'I'd like it put between me and that maniac Truman, please.'

I am not replying on behalf of Yorkshire cricket, but I am replying on behalf of your guests. We really do appreciate your hospitality tonight, and we appreciate all the kind things that you said about us. This is the fourth Association dinner that I have attended, and each one is better than the one before. As Chairman of the Tourist Authority I know something about hospitality and tonight really has been exceptional.

My wife joins me in saying this. Unfortunately, etiquette prevents her saying that her book is published locally, costs £14.99 and can be obtained next week from all good bookshops.

Ladies and gentlemen of the Association. Once again thank you from your guests. We hope to be with you next year. **9**

———— The toast to the ladies ————

This is normally given at a function of an organisation whose membership is exclusively male, and which holds periodic events to which women are invited. Freemasonry and rugby clubs provide two examples. As the number of men only organisations is declining, so too is the number of times that a toast to the women is proposed. Nevertheless, it remains a common after dinner toast at social functions. The toast is sometimes proposed by a young single man, but this is by no means always the case.

There is a terrible trap into which many men have fallen when proposing this toast. The speaker should not be condescending or patronising. He should most definitely avoid:

- references to the women's role in making the sandwiches
- an implication that women would not be able to manage the activity carried out by the host organisation

- a thank you to the women for letting their menfolk attend the all-male meetings. This antagonises both men and women
- most sexist humour, though it some cases it can be effective. It is a very high risk strategy.

On the last point, I once heard a speaker tell of a meeting between a very intelligent man, a very intelligent woman, and Father Christmas. The lights went out and when they came back on a £10 note was missing. The speaker asked who had taken it and said that there was a logical answer and it was possible to work it out.

After a pause he said that the money had been taken by the very intelligent man. This was logical because the other two did not exist. This piece of humour was received in stony silence. However, it might have worked if he had turned it round and said that it had been taken by the very intelligent woman.

The speech should praise the women present. It may flatter but should not go over the top. Sincere praise is often the most effective. As with all after dinner toasts, humour is often appreciated.

Specimen toast to the ladies

- **TIME** *2–2¹/₂ minutes*

  ❝ Every member of this club has been eagerly looking forward to tonight's dinner and dance. There are of course several reasons for this, but one of the main ones is that it is our Ladies' Night. Have we ever had a happier gathering than tonight? I do not think so.

  We are an all-male club, and I know that some of the ladies are not always too sure exactly what we do all the time. Well, I will let you into a secret. Every so often we have a discussion about how much we appreciate you and what we can do to make life pleasant for you.

  Some of our members go to great lengths. A few years ago we had a member who was deaf and dumb. He thought so much of his wife that he decided to always wear boxing gloves in bed. It was because he had bad dreams that led to him talking in his sleep.

  As well as welcoming you tonight I want to take the opportunity of thanking you for your support and tolerance during the year. We do really appreciate it.

Now! members of the club. Please join me in drinking the toasts to the ladies. **9**

Specimen reply to the toast to the ladies

- **TIME** *2–2¹/₂ minutes*

6 On behalf of the ladies I would like to thank you for the most generous toast, and to tell you that we are honoured by the compliments that you paid us.

You have a very high opinion of we ladies. I can only think that I was asked to reply because I come from a family that has an equally high opinion of men. Yes, it is true. We all do. Take my Aunty Molly for instance. She is eighty-four and she still thinks highly of men.

Aunty Molly never misses the evening services at our church. And last Sunday the vicar recognised this support with a nice little gesture. He said that the choir was available to her and that she could choose any hymn that she liked. Aunty Molly took a close look at the choir, then said thank you very much and that she would choose **him** on the end.

Yes! it is true. We ladies do support your work throughout the year, and we are pleased to do so. Once again, thank you for your hospitality tonight and thank you for your very kind toast. **9**

SUMMARY

1 Get the length of the speech right. Do not speak for too long.
2 The audience will nearly always appreciate humour.
3 The audience will always appreciate sincerity.
4 At all costs do not be boring. Put some interest and excitement into the content.
5 Avoid excessive eating and drinking prior to speaking.
6 Make sure that your voice is heard.
7 Try to be topical. It is very good for a responder to a toast to refer to something that has just been said.

11

SPEECHES AT SPORTING OCCASIONS

These are a special type of the after dinner speeches and toasts described in the last chapter. It is well worth reading through Chapter 10 as preparation for this topic. All the advice applies to speeches at sporting occasions. The following is a short summary of some of the key points in that chapter:

- Get the timing right. Do not speak for too long.
- Humour will be appreciated.
- Do not eat or drink to excess prior to speaking.
- Make sure that you can be heard. Move your speaking position if necessary.
- Above all else, do not be boring.

Humour is likely to be appreciated in many speeches, but never more so than when the speech is delivered to a sporting audience. At some events it is virtually demanded, so it is worth paying particular attention to this aspect of the speech. The audience may well be in a boisterous mood and very receptive to jokes. Occasions such as these lend themselves to good-natured jibes at the expense of traditional rivals.

Also appropriate are generous tributes to the skill and sportsmanship of opponents, particularly if they are present. This may, for example, be at a dinner for the teams after a fixture.

The remainder of this chapter introduces the most common sporting toasts and gives some specimen examples.

— The Club, The Association, etc —

This has many similarities with the toast to the organisation discussed in the last chapter. It may be to a particular club (e.g. Arsenal Football Club) or to a wider body (e.g. The Football Association).

Specimen toast to Arsenal Football Club

● **TIME** *3¹/₂–4¹/₂ minutes*

❝ I follow the two best football teams in Britain, Arsenal and Arsenal Reserves. And tonight it is my pleasure to propose a toast to a great football club, The Arsenal. A great football club. That statement can be made in the past, present and future tenses.

Our past is unrivalled, and we have a trophy cabinet to prove it. Name a dozen great British players of the past and I'm sure that one or two would be Arsenal players. What about great managers? Surely Herbert Chapman would be top of most lists. And you would have to include Tom Whittaker and Bertie Mee, and others as well.

The present is good too. We have a first-rate team and the place is bubbling with enthusiasm. And as for the future, well one look at the youth team answers that question. In a few years time they will be world beaters.

Ladies and gentlemen, no toast to Arsenal Football Club would be complete without a word of sympathy for our good neighbours Tottenham Hotspur. Here is an intellectual question for you. Why is the Star of David like Tottenham Hotspur? (pause) It is because both have got six points.

A lawyer friend of mine told me that they even got a mention in court last week. It was a child custody case and as is often the way the judge awarded custody to the mother. But the boy in question was most upset and shouted out 'I don't want to live with my mother. She beats me'. The judge was a kindly man so he changed his mind and ordered that the little boy live with his father.

But this was not right either. The little boy shouted out 'I don't want to live with my father. He beats me'. The judge was terribly upset and he asked the boy if there was anyone he would like to live with, perhaps his grandmother. 'I want to live with Tottenham Hotspur,' replied the little chap. 'They don't beat anybody.'

But let me return to the subject of my toast. What other football club is so liked and so respected that people put **The** before its name? Do people talk about **The** Everton or **The** Wimbledon. No! But they do say **The** Arsenal.

And my toast tonight is to a very great football club. Would you please raise your glasses and drink a toast to **The** Arsenal. ❯

As readers may know, Tottenham Hotspur is the traditional North London rival of Arsenal. The joke about the Star of David was popular some years ago when Tottenham Hotspur made a very bad start to the season. They lost several matches in a row and for some time were bottom of the division with just six points. Like most sports jokes, the ones in this speech can be adapted and a different team substituted.

Not many people propose a toast to the mighty Arsenal, but the formula works as well for a more humble sporting body.

Specimen toast to the Rutland County Golf Club

● **TIME** *3–3¹/₂ minutes*

❮ General MacArthur said that old soldiers never die; they simply fade away. Had he been talking about golfers he might have said that old golfers never die; they simply lose their balls.

I am an old golfer and very proud of it. And being an old golfer I have had the privilege of playing at many clubs, and not just in this country. I have enjoyed them all, but it has made me realise just what a marvellous club we have here at Rutland County.

For a start there is the beauty of the setting. Never mind the golf, I would drive fifty miles just to look at the scenery.

And the course itself is one of the most interesting. Not the hardest, but I never play a round without seeing a different aspect to it.

But best of all there is you, the members. You are a smashing group, both in golfing terms and on the social side as well. I am fortunate to serve as your chairman, and I am fortunate to have the support of such a good committee. I would like to mention them all by name and tell you just what they do for the club. Time prohibits that, but I will just mention the hard work of Paul Bates our secretary. I know that we are all looking forward to hearing him soon.

A minute ago I said that I was an old golfer, and I would like to think that I have learned something over the years. When I started I thought that if you were hit by a flying golf ball and then heard a shout of 'fore', it meant that there were three more balls on the way.

Whether or not I have increased my knowledge of golf I have certainly developed my appreciation of this great club. And that ladies and gentlemen is my toast. Would you please be upstanding and drink a toast to the Rutland County Golf Club. **9**

Specimen reply to the toast to the Rutland County Golf Club to be given by the Secretary

- **TIME** *3¹/₂–4¹/₂ minutes*

6 I think that we can all identify with what Tom has just said. I must admit that I am struggling over the tribute to the Secretary, but I suppose that I do know what he means, and I think that his remarks will definitely grow on me. But what he said about the rest of the committee was spot on, and what he said about the members too.

On behalf of the club, and of the members, I would like to thank you for your generous remarks. And I would like to add one of my own. There is one committee member who you did not mention by name, a man who does a vast amount of work for the club. He is a man who has been a dedicated member for many years, and who is nearly at the end of an outstanding year in office. I am of course referring to none other than our Chairman Tom Green. Thank you Tom.

A club Secretary does not often get the chance to give an audience his personal views, but I am going to take this opportunity to raise an issue that causes me great alarm. I refer to the growth of gambling in our game of golf. We can accept it in inferior sports such as racing and football, even in cricket. But do we really want it in the glorious game of golf?

The problem is that it can take over a person's whole life. Take a friend of mine. He placed six bets a day, every single day for a whole year. And do you know, not a single one of those bets won anything. He was the world's unluckiest gambler.

It was so bad that even the bookmaker was sorry for him. So at the end of the year he fixed a bet that even my friend could not lose. The bookmaker took his hat and he put into it a £5 note, a £20 note and a £50 note. My friend had to put his hand in the hat and take one out. He could not lose and he had to win either £5, £20 or £50. My friend put in his hand and do you know what he won? Something that said six and seven-eighths.

So! let's keep gambling out of golf. And that's quite enough from your Secretary. Mr Chairman, I thank you for your toast. **9**

Our opponents

A frequently encountered toast is to the opposing team or to 'Our Opponents'. This is sometimes proposed at a dinner for the teams and officials following an important match, or following a fixture with a great tradition. Examples are the Oxford and Cambridge Boat Race, and various rugby internationals.

As well as these renowned fixtures it is often proposed following matches of local interest. The following toast is set following a mythical baseball game in the U.S.A.

Specimen toast to Cougar Valley Baseball Club

● **TIME** *1¹/₂–2 minutes*

6 This afternoon we played our forty-seventh fixture against our friends from Cougar Valley. They have won a few more than us, but we narrowly won today. So honours are about even.

We always enjoy the match and it is always a keen game played in a very sporting spirit. And today was no exception. We enjoy most of our games but the Cougar Valley match is always something special.

Before closing I must pay tribute to a great pitching performance by Mark Caplan, and also to the captaincy of Ben Hughes. Things were so tight out there that I know you are not going to lose many matches this season.

Ben, it is my pleasure to propose the toast to you, your players and supporters. Ladies and gentlemen of Bird Valley, would you please drink a toast to the Cougar Valley Baseball Club. **❯**

This toast is often short and pays tribute to the sportsmanship and skill of the other team. The response follows a similar style.

The Captain

Often a toast is proposed to honour the captain of a team. Sometimes it is a stand-alone toast, and sometimes it is coupled with another one, such as the club. It may for example be 'West Thornton Cricket Club coupled with the Name of the Captain, Jack Jarvis'.

An essential element is a tribute to the captain's hard word and the skills that he or she has brought to the task. Presumably the captain has many admirable qualities that can be praised, and this can be done up to the limit. On the other hand overpraise should be avoided. As with all sporting toasts, humour will be appreciated.

The captain's reply should not be too long, will probably be relatively modest, and will usually give credit to the club and the team.

Specimen toast to The Captain of Romford Wanderers Football Club

● **TIME** *2¹/₂–3 minutes*

❮ Just what does a captain do? According to the great Danny Blanchflower, captain of Tottenham Hotspur and Northern Ireland, not much. He said that at five minutes to three he picked up the ball and said 'Let's get stuck into this lot'. At one minute to three he called 'heads', and if he was right elected to kick the way the wind was blowing. And that was absolutely all that he ever did as captain. All the praise of his captaincy was completely undeserved.

Well all I can say is that Danny Blanchflower never met Billy Jones. If Billy had been captaining Tottenham Hotspur they would have done the double every year, not just once.

This club has been fortunate to have Billy Jones as captain for the whole of last season. We did not win any trophies but it was a good season. And a good part of the reason was Billy's hard work and inspired leadership. He always set the example.

To take one instance he was nearly always on the training pitch five minutes before anyone else. His leadership on the field was exceptional and I have never known a captain give more encouragement to the younger players. We have several good youngsters in the team now and Billy has brought them on faster than anyone would have believed possible.

So! Congratulations on a good season, Billy, and thanks for all you have done. And here's to the next campaign, when we confidently expect our captain to be presented with the Division 2 Trophy at the end of the season. Ladies and gentlemen, the toast is to The Captain. **9**

Specimen reply to the toast to The Captain of Romford Wanderers Football Club

● **TIME** 2½–3 minutes

6 The secret of being a good captain is having a loyal team on the pitch, and a good set of workers supporting the club behind the scenes. I think that is probably what Danny Blanchflower meant to say. Here at Romford Wanderers we have exactly that. No captain could have asked for more support than I received last season.

In thanking you for this toast, I want to share the honour with my Vice-Captain Jim, and with all seventeen players who turned out during the season. And of course with all the people who helped in other ways.

I am of course very much aware of the responsibilities of being captain. Loyal supporters may sometimes blindly follow their captain against their better judgement.

As a warning I try to remember something that happened to the American President Calvin Coolidge. He was entertaining a group of about fifty supporters to afternoon tea in the White House. After tea had been poured the President transferred his from the cup to his saucer. As I said they were loyal supporters who felt that they should behave in the same way as their President. So all fifty guests poured their tea into their saucers. The President then put his saucer on the floor for the cat.

Once again, my thanks to everyone who has given me such great support this season. Please keep it up next season and we'll see if we can have a trophy on the mantelpiece by this time next year. ❯

SUMMARY

1 At this of all times, do not be boring.
2 Do not speak for too long.
3 Keep a light touch.
4 Humour is almost demanded. A good-natured joke at the expense of traditional rivals may be well received.
5 Share the praise with others and with the club as a whole.
6 Sincere tributes to opponents are often required.
7 Do not forget to thank the back-room workers who help the club.

12

PRESENTATION OF PRIZES AT A SCHOOL SPEECH DAY

You probably recall this part of your schooldays with very mixed feelings. Memories may well include rather long, rather patronising and rather boring speeches, all delivered by seemingly elderly men and women. In reality these worthy people were probably aged about forty and they probably spoke for around ten minutes. On the other hand some of the speeches may have been lively, interesting, relevant and memorable. It is thirty-five years on, but I would like to pay a belated tribute to Mr Roberton, a music publisher from Wendover, who enlivened my schooldays with such a speech.

It is important to consider carefully the composition of the audience and the appropriate tone to adopt. The audience will include many 'children', but there will also be teachers and probably parents as well. If it is a secondary school some of the pupils will be up to eighteen years old.

It is probably best to make the tone of the speech similar to one you would use if addressing a group of young adults. Take particular care to make your presentation lively. This is always important, but never more so than with this assignment. The audience's attention span may be slightly shorter than with mature adults. So make it lively, make it strong, make it memorable, and do not make it too long. It is almost essential that you ask the school in advance about the right length of the speech. However, perhaps five to ten minutes may be about right.

On no account should you be patronising. Remember that teenagers have an unrivalled talent to feel patronised, even when it is not intended and no reasonable adult can see it. On no account describe the audience as children. I would start the speech with 'Headmaster, ladies and gentlemen', and certainly not with 'Headmaster, boys and girls'.

It is usually a mistake to adopt a style of dress very different from your normal style. Do look smart and do look modern, but leave teenage dress to the teenagers. Similarly, use a good lively style of speech, but do not overindulge in teenage slang. Excesses in dress and speech can make you seem insincere. It is not unknown for certain Ministers of Religion to fall into these traps.

It may be appropriate to bring one or two statistics into your speech. This will be in order to praise the achievements of the prize winners, or to draw attention to a particularly fine achievement of the school. It may be a good idea, indeed it may be virtually demanded, but it should be done with care. Use just one or two statistics and bring them in with a light touch. The audience will only be able to assimilate one or two. The place for anything more detailed is in a written report.

For example, suppose the school has a particularly good record in teaching the French language. It would be effective to say the following:

❛ Modern languages are so important. As a representative of a big exporter I know just how much the country needs those skills. So headmaster, I am delighted to congratulate the school on its exceptional success in teaching the French language. Last year over ninety per cent of sixteen-year-olds got A to C grades in GCSE French. The national average is under half, so it really is quite an achievement. ❜

The same point will send the audience to sleep if it is put in the following way:

❛ Last year 56.1 per cent of sixteen-year-old pupils got grade A French in their GCSE. A further 13.5 per cent got grade B and 21.2 per cent got grade C. So overall 90.8 per cent got grades A to C. But of course 2.9 per cent of girls and 1.6 per cent of boys took the exam last year and got grades A, B or C. So after allowing for this, 95.3 per cent got the grades. And three pupils could not sit the exam because they were ill, and allowing for this it becomes 96.1 per cent. Last year it was 84.9 per cent, but that was before the adjustment of course. ❜

You probably did not manage to read right through this and the audience will not follow it either. So keep statistics short and simple.

It is a good idea to praise the school and try to send everyone away feeling good about it. Pick out one or two very positive points and praise them. This may include its academic record, or some part of it, but may also include one or two wider points. Whilst praising the school's non-academic and caring side, on no account should you seem to belittle the achievement of the prize winners. The main point of the day is to honour their achievement and hard work.

You may well have a central theme to your speech. For example a businessman might talk about career opportunities awaiting. A bishop might want to talk about ethical standards and the obligation to be of service.

As with almost all speeches, humour and a light touch will almost certainly be welcomed. The audience will probably appreciate one or two anecdotes, provided that they are interesting and relevant.

I attended Aylesbury Grammar School from 1955–60. The following speech is the one that I might give if now invited to present prizes at that school. The school is a large, successful, boy's grammar school, though when I attended it was co-educational.

Specimen speech on presentation of prizes at the speech day of Aylesbury Grammar School

- **TIME** *6-7¹/₂ minutes*

  ❻ Headmaster, ladies and gentlemen.

  I was greatly honoured by your invitation to present the prizes today. I several times wondered, why me? apart from the fact that I do not charge a fee. Perhaps it is because my very high regard for the school is known. And perhaps the fact that I am an old boy of the school had something to do with it.

  Yes, it's true. I first came here in 1955, wearing short trousers. Boys did in those days. It's so long ago that Pontius was still a pilot. Mr Tidmarsh was the Headmaster, a very respected man; known for making a temporary impression at one end and a permanent impression at the other.

Continuity has always been a feature of this great school. Mr Tidmarsh was one of only six headmasters this century. Some football teams have more managers in one season.

One or two careers have spanned a very long time indeed. Mr Deeming was the senior master when I was at the school. He came in 1919 and spent his entire career here. In the early days he ran swimming classes in the canal, and remembered the boys from the villages riding to school on horseback. They stabled them for the day at the Wheelwright Arms in Walton Road.

They were great days and we had some things that you don't have now. Girls for one thing. Two-course lunches for nine pence, old money, for another. But you have so many good things that we never had – the language laboratories, the swimming pool, and a better teacher/pupils ratio. And of course, twice as many pupils – all boys, though; shame about that.

And I must congratulate you all on the school's academic achievement. The record really is outstanding. Twenty-three successes for Oxford and Cambridge, and such a high overall standard in the exams.

I know that averages can be misleading. You probably know of the man who stood with one foot in a bath of scalding water. The other foot was in a bucket of ice. So on average he was comfortable. But however you interpret the averages in those published league tables, Aylesbury Grammar has beaten them, and it is right up there near the top. By the way, the man who had his foot in the ice bucket was a masochist. He loved cold baths (pause) so every day he had a hot one.

I joke about the exams, but perhaps I should not, because the splendid results did not just happen. They were the result of a lot of hard work, by the teachers and also of course by the people who took them. I congratulate you all.

Headmaster, you can take pride in things other than the exams. I could give dozens of examples but just two will suffice. The rugby team was undefeated all last season, and the school raised £8,000 for the Mayor's charity appeal. A staggering achievement. Well done!

I represented local industry on the Mayor's committee, and that brings me on to what I think was probably your main reason for inviting me here today. I am representing industry here now, and I bring a message from industry for you. The country needs the high standards that you achieve in this school.

International competition gets tougher every year and we have to keep up with it. Of course we intend to do more than that. We intend to move ahead of it and there is work to be done. There certainly is in my company and it's true of others as well. There are some very good careers waiting for you, and I believe that it is work with a high social value. The country can only spend what it earns. By helping to create the wealth you will be providing the resources to help the less fortunate.

That seems an excellent point at which to conclude, so I will now once again give my heartiest congratulations to all the prize winners, and move on to present the prizes. **9**

SUMMARY

1 Ask the school for guidance about the length of your speech.
2 Adopt the right tone; perhaps as though speaking to young adults.
3 Do not be patronising.
4 Praise the school and praise the prize winners. Send them home feeling good.
5 Humour is good and a few relevant anecdotes are good. Make the presentation lively.
6 Make the statistics short, simple and infrequent.

13

SPEAKING TO A CLUB OR ORGANISATION

This chapter encompasses a wide variety of speaking invitations. You may be asked to speak to a dozen or so people in a small room. At the other extreme there could be hundreds of people, with the event being held in a large hall. Particularly challenging, and occasionally encountered, is an event with a very small audience gathered in one corner of a very large hall.

A successful speech to a club or organisation depends on a whole range of considerations, and many of them were studied in the first part of this book. Time spent reading this section is an excellent investment. It will help with all the speaking assignments, but none more so than this one. If you have turned straight to this chapter, please seriously consider reading the first section of the book before going any further.

A very good starting point is to consider the likely motivation of the people who have invited you to speak. You should then think about your own motivation in accepting the invitation. The reasons may be entirely compatible but this will not necessarily be the case. You should always be very clear in your own mind about your objectives in speaking, whether or not they clash with anyone else's objectives. You will then be much more likely to achieve your aims.

Perhaps the most common reason for an invitation is that a group of people wish to spend an enjoyable period of time together, typically half an hour, or an hour or so. They probably hope to be informed on an interesting subject, and to be entertained. It may not be admitted but entertainment could well be the higher priority. They certainly want to go home having had a good time. You may have been invited because you have a reputation as a good speaker, or you may have been invited because you are known to be knowledgeable in a particular field. Perhaps you have been invited because of your employment, or because of another organisation to which you belong. On the other hand, and let us be brutally honest about it, perhaps you have been invited because they are finding it difficult to get a speaker.

Your motivation in accepting may partly be a wish to help out. It may reflect your pride in having been asked. It may be a wish to accept a challenge and to obtain a sense of achievement in doing a good job. You may expect to enjoy preparing and delivering the talk. It is a characteristic of the human race that we all want to promote knowledge of subjects that interest us, and persuade others to our particular point of view. People who study the migratory habits of toads believe that the world would be a happier place if more people knew about the subject. This belief is of course entirely correct.

All the above is compatible with the preceding reasons for the invitation. Thought should, however, be given to a possible conflict if your main aim is to promote a particular product. A good analogy is the so-called television chat show. Everyone knows that many celebrities only appear because they want to plug their latest book. Everyone is happy, provided that the celebrity does it sparingly and with a light touch. The television station gets a good programme, the viewers are entertained, and the book is duly plugged. But it goes wrong if the celebrity goes too far and abuses the hospitality.

Let us suppose, for example, that you work for the Coca Cola Corporation and you have been invited to speak. It would be a good idea to talk mainly about such things as the discovery of the formula, how the secret is preserved, how the company resolved to make the product available to every G.I. during the war, and how the company helped bring the Olympic Games to Atlanta. This will, or should be, very interesting. Then at the end you could spend a minute or so saying that the drink continues to be marvellous value and is, in your opinion, the best drink in the world. Perhaps this could be introduced with a broad smile and the words, 'Now for a word from our sponsor'.

The following is a very abbreviated summary of some of the main points to remember.

- **Timing**   This is very important. Ask the organisers in advance how long they want. Then make your own judgement. Do not make it too long. Prepare slightly more than you expect to need, and have one or two self-contained sections that can be left out.

- **Humour**   This will nearly always improve the impact of the speech. As well as entertaining the audience it should make the serious points more memorable. This was covered in some detail in Chapter 4.

- **Anecdotes**   One or two well-chosen anecdotes, relevant and memorable, can be the high points of a speech. They can certainly make it memorable and may well be worth including. This too was covered in detail in Chapter 4.

- **Technical terms, statistics and jargon**   These are the ruin of many otherwise good speeches. Technical terms and statistics should be used sparingly. Jargon should not be used at all. Do not overestimate the audience's ability to absorb technical terms and statistics. It is a very common mistake. If the detail is very important, make the speech simple and give all the details in a written handout.

- **Topical references**   Do not be afraid to depart from your script and say something topical. Perhaps something in the day's news is relevant to your speech. The audience will probably respect you for referring to it.

- **Speak with authority**   This is partly a matter of confidence. You will sound confident if you are confident. You will be much more confident if you know that you have prepared thoroughly and checked your facts. Do not let the audience catch you out over a mistake with the facts, especially if you are speaking as an expert. Authority also depends on the way that you speak and this was covered in detail in Chapter 6.

- **Relate your speech to the audience**   You may have an extremely good standard speech, but it will be better still if you can relate it to a particular group of people. If your speech is about the need for good public libraries, for example, try to show how a good library would benefit this particular town and this particular group of people.

- **Visual aids**   A few really good visual aids can enormously enhance the impact of a speech. If used badly they can ruin it. Remember always to talk to the audience and not to the visual aid. Many visual aids are too small and too fussy. Make yours big and simple. Make a last minute check of the visual aid before speaking.

Visual aids were covered in detail in Chapter 7.

- **Questions**   You may want to terminate your speech with a question and answer session. This is often a very good idea and it can enhance your presentation. It has a useful side benefit when there is a lot of time to be filled as it uses up some time without the need for preparation. Keep in mind the following:
  - You cannot possibly know the answer to every question that may be asked. Do not prevaricate, especially if there is danger that you may be found out. Either say that you do not know or that you will find out and provide the answer later.
  - Questions are often mumbled by people not facing the audience. If it is not clear repeat the question loudly for the audience.
  - Repeating the question is a good way of gaining time to think of the answer.
  - Do not make your answers too long.
  - Try and establish a rapport with the audience and with questioners. Do not insult a questioner, even if it is a silly question.
  - If it is a long, rambling question, paraphrase it for the audience.
  - It can be amusing and effective to give a one word answer (yes or no) to a long rambling question.
  - Do not finish just by answering the last question. Say something that sums up your whole presentation.

There is an almost infinite number of clubs and organisations and therefore an almost infinite number of possible speeches. Also, the speeches are usually longer than can comfortably be fitted into this chapter. For these reasons no whole specimen speeches are given. Instead, examples of different parts of a speech are studied. All the following extracts are based on a hypothetical talk about Gilbert and Sullivan, the English couple who wrote and composed the much-loved nineteenth-century light operas.

—— Examples of effective openings ——

❛ Have you noticed that an audience will always enthusiastically applaud any performance of a Gilbert and Sullivan light opera? No matter if it is an inept performance. No matter if the singers are out of tune. There is always warm applause. Why should

this be? There would not be the same response to a bad performance of an Arthur Miller play. The answer, ladies and
gentlemen, is because the performers are almost irrelevant. The
audience is applauding the genius and the personalities of the
writer and the composer. Gilbert and Sullivan – the subject of
my talk tonight. **❯**

This is an effective opening, because it is intriguing and will engage
the audience's attention. They will work out if it is true and be
interested in what is to follow. And yes readers, it is true. If you go to
a performance of a Gilbert and Sullivan opera you may observe the
phenomenon.

❮ Some names are forever grouped together in peoples' minds.
Marks and Spencer, Laurel and Hardy, fish and chips.

Gilbert and Sullivan come into this category. Each was famous
in his own right. Gilbert the barrister and talented writer.
Sullivan the gifted composer. But the collaboration was so much
greater than the sum of the parts. Together they were Gilbert
and Sullivan, a partnership of genius. **❯**

This too is interesting and sets the scene for the talk that is to follow.

_____ Example of good speech _____
construction

There are many, many, possibilities but this is one possible outline of
a successful talk:

- chosen opening
- Gilbert prior to collaboration
- Sullivan prior to collaboration
- their meeting and first work together
- the great light operas
- success and public acclaim
- how they worked together
- their quarrel
- just why were they so successful?
- chosen ending.

———— **Examples of highlights** ————

The above outline is one example of a logical construction, but this is not enough. Very few people go home and tell their partners, 'I heard a really well-constructed speech tonight'. Speech construction is nevertheless important and the basis for everything else. People do go home and tell their partners, 'I heard something amazing tonight'. Or they may say, 'I heard such an interesting story'. They also remember and recount something humorous.

You should aim to give your talk highlights. This could be in the form of really good anecdotes, the introduction of a surprise, the use of memorable phrases and especially the use of humour. All this was covered in detail in Chapter 4. The following are some examples:

❦ We sometimes think that stinging satire is an invention of the twentieth century. But consider these lines from *HMS Pinafore*:

I grew so rich that I was sent
By a pocket borough into parliament
I always voted at my party's call
And I never thought of thinking for myself at all
I thought so little they rewarded me
By making me the ruler of the Queen's navee.

The character is Sir Joseph Porter KCB. Gilbert based him on W. H. Smith, the founder of the famous chain of newsagents. But he was also a politician and Disraeli's First Lord of the Admiralty. He was said to have little knowledge of naval affairs. ❧

This is funny, and funnier still if you can manage to sing it. The name W. H. Smith introduces an element of surprise. A British audience would be bound to find it very interesting indeed. Here is something similar, though without the quotation.

❦ There is something in the human condition that makes many popular entertainers wish to be known for their serious work. Comedians are notorious for wanting to play Hamlet.

It famously afflicted Conan Doyle who was forever trying to kill off Sherlock Holmes so that he could concentrate on his serious work. Sullivan's gifts extended to a whole range of music and he was often tempted to concentrate on his classical work. No less a person than Queen Victoria urged this course upon him. Perhaps, to coin a phrase, 'She was not amused'. **9**

—— **Example of effective ending** ——

Speech endings were examined in some detail in Chapter 3. The following is an example of how the speech could be summed up in a few phrases with a tribute to the great couple.

6 It would have been terrible if they had died without making up their quarrel, but happily, in time, they were reconciled. Sullivan died soon afterwards. Gilbert lived on until 1911 when, at the age of 75, he tragically drowned in a bizarre accident in a garden swimming pool in Pinner.

They were great Victorians and the world was happier for their partnership. They enriched our culture. They made us laugh. They left a thousand witty phrases and a hundred memorable tunes. We shall not see their like again. **9**

SUMMARY

1 If you have not read the opening chapters of this book you should consider doing so.
2 Think about why you have been asked. Then be clear why you have accepted.
3 Take the timing seriously.
4 Work out the construction, then put in the highlights.
5 Highlights help make the serious parts digestible.
6 Most audiences want to be entertained.
7 Be ruthless with statistics, technical terms and jargon.
8 A good question and answer session may well enhance the presentation.

14

SPEAKING AT A FUND-RAISING EVENT

This, of course, largely consists of raising money for charity, though money is sometimes raised for good causes that do not quite fit the definition of charity. Your speech should first of all be an effective one according to the general principles explained in this book but fund raising is a specialised task, and there are a number of points to which you should pay particular attention.

In making the speech you will probably have three main aims:

- Firstly you will want to raise as large a sum as possible. This is one of the rare occasions where you will be able to measure your success exactly. Following an after dinner speech you will probably ask yourself how well it was received. Friends may say it was very good, but perhaps they are being kind and their words should be discounted. If it is a fund-raising speech you can at least measure the funds raised. If last year's speaker raised £2,000, you set out to get £3,000, and you actually got £4,000, then you have done well, at least by this criterion.
- Money is important but it is not everything. You will want the audience to gain an understanding of the work of the charity. You will also want them to go home with favourable views of the charity and its officials. Perhaps this greater understanding will bring non-financial benefits. For example, an employer may attend a fund-raising talk for a charity that helps people suffering from a particular disability. He may as a result resolve to help provide employment for a person with a particular handicap.
- As always, you will have the personal motive of doing well for

yourself. We all want to sit down thinking that we have done a first-rate job and are highly regarded by the listeners.

The following are some of the points that should receive your special attention when delivering a fund-raising speech.

1 Make sure that your speech conveys sincerity

An audience always values sincerity, but never more so than when they are asked to contribute to a good cause. They want to believe that the speaker sincerely believes what he is saying. A sincere person who is not absolutely proficient in his technique may do better than a slick operator who is technically faultless, but leaves the audience wondering if it is all a performance.

The best advice for appearing sincere is to be sincere. If this is not possible perhaps you should abandon the task, and find a cause to which you can give unqualified support.

Assuming that you are sincere, let it show and speak from the heart. Someone with personal experience is particularly well placed to show sincerity. Perhaps this could be a person who has been helped by the charity, or a relative of a person who has been helped.

2 Make sure that the audience is thinking of a realistic contribution

This advice is very mercenary but also very practical. Some salesmen put a copy of the contract on the desk as soon as they meet a client. This is a way of ensuring that the client keeps in mind the object of the visit. Similarly, a fund raiser may introduce realistic sums into his speech. Consider the following:

❻ The new hospital equipment costs £100,000 and we have all pledged ourselves to raise £5,000 tonight. I am delighted to tell you that we have made a wonderful start. Club funds will contribute £1,000 and one of your members has kindly sent me £100 in advance of tonight's meeting. During dinner four people each gave me cheques for £50.

So, ladies and gentlemen, we have a great start – £1,300 in all. Now I am asking you to make up the rest. ❾

The listeners have heard mention of £1,000, £100, and four contributions of £50. This will have implanted in their minds that £50 is some sort of norm. They will want to think themselves as generous as their friends, and may have this in mind when they make their contribution.

Note also that people like to be associated with a winning appeal. They may give more generously when they know that a good start has been made. For this reason it may be a good idea to announce contributions pledged in advance. Organisers of such events as Comic Relief know this when they say at the beginning that the total pledged exceeds two million pounds, or some such figure.

3 Show that the money is getting through to the intended beneficiaries

Many people are suspicious that too high a proportion of money donated does not get through to the main charitable purpose. They may believe that too much is taken by headquarters, expenses, cost of appeals and, worst of all, commission for fund raisers.

Unfortunately, they may have good reason for these fears.

If your expenses ratio is high you have a problem. If it is low you may like to stress this point in your speech. Consider the following:

❛ I know that many of you will be considering a donation of £10. If you are, please do something for me now. Get out your cheque book and write out a cheque for £10.40.

Why do I ask for the rather curious sum of £10.40? It's because our expenses and fund-raising costs are exactly four per cent of our income, and we are very proud that it is such a low figure.

So will you consider a cheque for £10.40? Forty pence will pay the bills and the whole £10 will go to Africa, and be spent on our hospital there.

Thank you so much. Now I am going to ask you to do something else. Will you write out a cheque for £10.35 and date it one year from today? That's right. I am asking for less next year. We are working on our expenses and we are going to get them down to just three and a half per cent. ❜

Another way of making the same point is the following:

❛ Your chairman was kind enough to reserve me a parking space, but you may have noticed that I did not use it. We do not have cars.

I mention this for two reasons. First of all because I need a lift to the station afterwards. But more importantly, because I want you to know that your contributions are not wasted. The maximum possible does go to buy lifeboats. ❜

4 Show emotion – but not too much

A charitable appeal is an emotional thing. The money is needed for a good cause. It is therefore permissible, as well as natural and desirable, to show some emotion about the need for the money, and how it is going to be spent.

Do not be afraid to show emotion, but do not go over the top. Do not fall into the trap of appearing manipulative and false. Take a warning from all those terrible show business awards where the winners say that they are astonished to have won (not true), are not worthy winners (probably true), and in any case owe it all to someone else. It is quite normal for the show business personalities to appear overcome with emotion whilst accepting the award, but the television viewers have their own ideas.

The following specimen speech illustrates these principles and some more as well. It is on behalf of CALIBRE, a small Aylesbury based charity that provides talking books for the blind.

Specimen fund-raising speech on behalf of CALIBRE

● **TIME** *5–6 minutes*

❧ I am sure that you have two questions in your mind. What exactly does CALIBRE do and is it really necessary? If you will give me a minute of your time I will answer those questions.

Please close your eyes and keep them closed for exactly a minute. Do not speak and I will tell you when the minute is up.

(A MINUTE OF SILENCE IS TIMED)

Thank you. You can open your eyes now. That is what it is like to be blind for a minute, but I want you to imagine being blind for ever. Perhaps you are blessed with a good family and many friends. But you will still be spending several hours each day alone, and in darkness.

CALIBRE helps fill those hours. One of the pleasures in life is visiting a library or bookshop and choosing a good book to read. CALIBRE gives that pleasure to the blind. The books are on tape and they are read by volunteer readers. CALIBRE is a cassette library and we have hundreds of books on tape. More

SPEAKING AT A FUND-RAISING EVENT

than 13,000 visually handicapped men and women use our services.

We are a small charity and we run on a shoestring. We can only operate because of the generosity of three groups of people.

Firstly, there is the Post Office. It delivers all our cassettes absolutely free and I pay tribute to it. We could not exist without this help.

Secondly, we are helped by 250 marvellous volunteers, including the people who read the books onto the cassettes. They only claim expenses, no salaries.

And thirdly, there are the people who donate funds to help our work. We are not government funded, and we are totally dependent on donations.

This, ladies and gentlemen, is what CALIBRE does and it is why I am asking for your help. We desperately need money. Each cassette costs £200 to make, and looking round the hall I am daring to hope that we could fund two new cassettes tonight. That would be £5 each.

Thank you for your time. CALIBRE is grateful for your help. I promise that it will not be wasted. **9**

There are other points to remember, among them these three:

1 Relate the charity to the particular audience
There is a well-known saying that charity should begin at home. You have probably heard people say that they prefer to give to local causes, or to people in the same trade. This is of dubious morality but it would be foolish to deny that it is a widespread attitude. If your appeal is for a local charity you might consider making sure that the point is fully realised. You might say something like the following:

6 We all know that Humberside has its fair share of the homeless, and that most of them are suffering through no fault of their own. I promise you that every penny raised tonight will be spent right here in Humberside. **9**

2 Make it interesting and enjoyable
If you only have two or three minutes, there is only time to grab attention, get across one or two key points and make an appeal for

a donation. If you have much longer the audience will expect a full and rounded speech, and it is up to you to give it to them. You cannot possibly spend half an hour just asking for money. You must make a speech about the charity, refer to the need for funds at one or two strategic points in it, and close with a strong appeal. Elsewhere in this book you were urged to send an audience home thinking that they have had a good time. This is true for a fund-raising speech too. Send them home feeling virtuous, and having had a good time. Humour may not be appropriate in a few charitable appeals, but is has a place in most of them.

3 Seize the moment

If your speech is a good one you will finish with the audience wanting to make a good donation. There may never be a better time to take the collection. People may go home fully intending to write out a cheque and post it at the weekend. Sadly, many of them, perhaps most of them, will not actually do it.

You should give your audience a chance to take action straight away. Pass round the plate at once.

The chapter is concluded with another example of a fund-raising speech, this time for a large nationally recognised charity. Note particularly the opening in the form of a question. This was one of the techniques mentioned in Chapter 3 and is a very good way of getting audience attention. The question is an interesting one which is discussed a great deal.

Specimen fund-raising speech on behalf of the NSPCC

- **TIME** *3¹/₂–4 minutes*

    ❛ Is child abuse on the increase? Or is it just that we hear more about it? We certainly do hear more about it, and we read more about it too. And I thank God that we do. It is only when we know about it, that we have a chance to do something about it.

    There is always damage but we can try to minimise it. We can try to start putting the pieces back together. I am speaking on behalf of an organisation that does just that. The NSPCC – The National Society for the Prevention of Cruelty to Children.

It's a name that you know, and you know something about the work that we do. For generations 'the man from the cruelty', as our inspectors are affectionately known, have worked to prevent children suffering and to help them when they do.

We are desperately needed in cases of physical child abuse, and of course especially in terrible cases of sexual abuse. And that is quite a lot of the work that we do. But is is by no means all. We do much more.

We fight cruelty to children in all its forms. Children suffer from ignorance as well as from deliberate cruelty. They suffer from neglect and they suffer from circumstances. Some of our work is to keep families together by means of support and education. It does not often make the headlines but it is expensive.

We would like to do more and I am afraid that there is more that needs to be done. And that is the reason why I am asking for your help. The British public is magnificent in the support that they give us and we desperately need every extra penny that we can get. The money that you give will all be spent on vital help for our children. Perhaps there is a child here in Newbury who will benefit from your generosity.

A few minutes ago I asked if child abuse is on the increase. Of course I do not know and neither does anyone else. But the NSPCC is fighting child abuse wherever it occurs – on the increase or not. Your help is desperately needed and I promise that it will be well used. Thank you for your generosity. **9**

SUMMARY

1 Be serious and realistic about the need to raise money. This is normally the prime purpose.
2 But do not go too far and alienate the audience. Money is not everything.
3 Make it interesting and perhaps bring in humour. It should be a good speech by several criteria. Give value for money.
4 Do not be afraid of emotion. But do not overdo it.
5 Try and relate the speech to the particular group of listeners.

15
INTRODUCING A SPEAKER

Any experienced speaker will attest that this is frequently done badly. It is worth looking at the most common faults in order that they may be avoided at all costs.

- It sometimes happens that the introducer gets one or more facts wrong. The audience may or may not notice, but the speaker certainly will. The name has to be correct. If the speaker is Celia Clegthorpe-Colman this is what must be said. Celia Clegthorpe-Colton will not do. Similarly, anything said about the speaker, the subject, or a related matter must be factually correct.
If in doubt you should check details in advance with the speaker. He is likely to be pleased that you have taken the trouble. It may also be a good idea to ask the speaker if there are any points that he would like mentioned in the introduction.
- It sometimes happens that the introducer speaks for an inappropriate period of time. This may be too long or too short, but too long is more common. If the time allocated to the speaker is extremely short, just three or four sentences is right. More usually one or two minutes may well be appropriate. If the speaker has been allocated fifteen or twenty minutes, it is usually wrong for the introducer to take more than a minute or two.
- It sometimes happens that the introducer displays excessive modesty and apologises for doing the job. He says that he is not worthy of the task of introducing such a fine speaker. This is bad. Even if you have a low opinion of yourself, you should not share it with the audience.
- It sometimes happens that the introducer steals the limelight of

the speaker. He makes a speech of his own, anticipating what the speaker is going to say. The introducer should always remember that the speaker is the star, and that his is only a supporting role.

● It sometimes happens that the introducer overpraises the speaker and sets expectations that cannot possibly be fulfilled. Even a good speaker may then cause the audience to think that he did not come up to expectations.

This is worst of all when the introducer promises the audience that the speaker is the funniest person on the face of the earth, and that they are in for a laugh a second. If the first joke falls flat the speaker is in for a hard time. It is right to praise the speaker, and to refer to his humour, but do not overdo it.

● It sometimes happens that the introducer is a bad speaker and mumbles platitudes. A speech of introduction has to be a good speech in its own right.

These are the traps to avoid. Now let us turn to a step-by-step approach towards constructing a successful speech of introduction.

The first step is to decide what facts will be brought into the speech, and if they are not to hand, get them. The one fact that is always essential is the name of the speaker. If in any doubt it should be written down and the phonetic pronunciation given too. The name of the former football manager could, for example, be written as BRIAN CLOUGH (PRONOUNCED CLUFF).

The next step is to think about a suitable time for the introduction. If the speaker's time is very short, so too should be the speech of introduction. Perhaps it should be as brief as the following:

❢ Ladies and gentlemen! We are fortunate to have with us Professor Marjorie Rowe. Professor Rowe is renowned for her knowledge of Inca Pottery and she will be talking to us on that subject. Would you please welcome Professor Rowe. ❢

For most speakers an appropriate introduction may well last for one or two minutes. If there is exceptionally detailed information to impart, more time may be taken. But, be hard on yourself. Do not speak for too long.

It is polite to have a word with the speaker in advance and ask if there are any points that he would particularly like made. Perhaps there is some special achievement that he would like drawn to the audience's attention. The speaker may be particularly grateful for the introducer preparing the audience for something that would otherwise interrupt the flow of his own speech. For example, if it is necessary for everyone to have paper and pencil ready, this could be called for in advance. This way a minute or so's disturbance can be got out of the way in advance.

If an opportunity occurs, do include something topical. The audience, and the speaker, will respect the inclusion of something that could not have been written a long time in advance. This could be something in the national or local news, or some relevant comment.

The style of speaking should always be friendly and welcoming. The subconscious message should be that the speaker is among friends who are going to make his visit enjoyable. The simultaneous message to the audience is that they are in for an enjoyable time.

This partly holds true for an occasion where the speaker holds views known to be contrary to those of the introducer and the group. An example would be the chairman of a company which wishes to build a chemical plant in an area where it is not wanted by most of the local people. In this case the introducer would thank the speaker for coming to state his case, and assure him of a fair hearing.

The main part of the introduction usually consists of information about the speaker and information about the subject. The proportions are a matter of individual choice.

It is important that the introduction builds up to a climax and does not just peter out. The best way of achieving this is to conclude with the name of the speaker, laying emphasis on the actual name at the very end of the sentence. For example 'Would you please welcome tonight's main speaker, **Charles Jenkins**'.

The chapter concludes with two examples of effective introductions. Both are in the one-to-two-minute time range, and they illustrate different points. The first example concentrates on the qualifications and experience of the speaker.

❝ It is my privilege to introduce our speaker, Professor William Brown. Professor Brown will be talking about modern trends in the teaching of mathematics, and as we all know, he is exceptionally qualified to do so.

He graduated from Cambridge with first class honours in 1981 and spent the next eight years at Harvard. He returned to Cambridge in 1989 and has done much to influence the teaching of mathematics in this country.

He served on the Goodchild Committee and has had several books published. The latest, entitled *Mathematics Beyond The Millennium*, was published earlier this year.

Ladies and gentlemen! Would you please welcome our guest speaker, **Professor William Brown**. ❯

The second example does not neglect the qualifications of the speaker, but concentrates on the subject. It shows the introducer preparing the audience as requested by the speaker.

❮ I am very pleased to introduce John Black who is going to tell us how this county was first mapped. John is known as a great expert on old maps and has studied the subject since he came to Cornwall eight years ago.

I am dying to know who made the first maps and how much they cost. And I am intrigued to know how accurate they were. In 1797 Dunstan Hill was said to be 831 feet high. Was it and how did they know?

You are going to be participating in a mapping experiment in a few minutes time so you will each need a pencil and a sheet of paper. Could you all make sure that you have them, please.

(SHORT PAUSE)

Thank you! Ladies and gentlemen I am delighted to introduce John Black. Please welcome **John Black**. ❯

SUMMARY

1 Always prepare thoroughly. Get the facts right. Above all, get the name right.
2 Remember that your role is secondary and that you are not the star.
3 Do not make a rival speech and do not speak for too long.
4 Do not so overpraise the speaker that the actual speech is an anticlimax.
5 Make one or two points about the speaker, the subject, or both.
6 Make the introduction friendly and welcoming.
7 Build up to a conclusion. End with the emphasis on the speaker's name.

16

PROPOSING A VOTE OF THANKS

Proposing a vote of thanks has a lot in common with delivering a speech that introduces a speaker. They top and tail the main event. It therefore follows that much of the advice in the last chapter can usefully be applied to a vote of thanks as well.

The first point is that the speaker should be thanked by name, and it is therefore essential that the name be mentioned, and be mentioned correctly. Similarly, any facts mentioned must also be correct. It may be nice to say that the speaker had great authority, enhanced by his nine years at Harvard. But this will not do if he spent twelve years at The Sorbonne, and it is even worse if the audience knows it because of the speech or the introduction . So the advice is, as it so often has been in this book, do your homework and get the facts right.

The advice about time in the last chapter also applies. If the speaker only has a short time, then a very short vote of thanks is suitable. In most cases a couple of minutes or so is probably about right. If it has been a very long speech then perhaps five minutes would be appropriate, unless the audience has become restive, in which case it should be shorter. Whatever the length of the vote of thanks, it should be the result of a deliberate decision, not something that just happens.

A vote of thanks should thank the speaker and normally praise him and the speech. This is right, but the praise should not be overdone. Excessive praise may well sound insincere and be counterproductive. This is especially true if the speech was not very good. In these circumstances it is probably wise to have rather more thanks and rather less praise. In any case do not appear unctuous and excessively humble.

The vote of thanks should sound warm and sincere. The best way to achieve sincerity is not to say anything not sincerely meant. Admittedly, this is a counsel of perfection, and good form may make it necessary to bend the truth a little. But this should be kept to a minimum.

The main point of a vote of thanks is to thank the speaker. So whatever is included or left out, this is essential. Remember to actually thank the speaker.

Much of the vote of thanks may be prepared in advance, perhaps all of it. However, be very conscious of the danger of the speaker doing something unexpected, or saying something that contradicts your prepared remarks. It is not associated with public speaking but take warning from the experience of Princess Elizabeth's former governess 'Crawfie'. She wrote reviews for a women's magazine of the 1955 Trooping the Colour and Royal Ascot. The magazine published the articles but unfortunately both events had been cancelled due to strikes. The articles had been written in advance and both she and the magazine looked ridiculous.

The public speaking equivalent is to prepare in advance and actually say that the speaker has been most interesting with his advice on growing cabbages. This might sound reasonable in the preparation, but would not be right if he had switched subjects and actually talked about the best way of pruning roses.

Even if the speech has been largely prepared in advance, it is good to say one or two things that indicate you have listened carefully. This conveys sincerity and enhances the vote of thanks. For example:

 ❦ We knew that Bill was an authority on the history of this town. But even so, we are in awe of the detail that he was able to bring to the talk. I am thinking in particular of the events leading up to the granting of the Royal Charter in 1589. His knowledge of that period is amazing. ❦

The main point of a vote of thanks is to thank the speaker and it is a good idea to make this the last thing said. It can therefore be the last thing that the speaker and the audience remember. It will probably be the first thing said as well. So the vote of thanks is often a sandwich construction with some detail between two thank yous.

You should aim to build up to a climax and end on a strong note. This may be with the final thank you, but often a vote of thanks is concluded with a round of applause. To make absolutely sure that the audience has taken the point you should yourself start to applaud. They will join in. The conclusion may be as follows:

❻ So once again John, thank you for a most entertaining and informative speech. We will show our appreciation in the usual way (leads applause). ❾

A specially delicate touch is required when the speaker has put forward controversial views. These may not necessarily be shared by the audience or the person delivering the thanks.

It is usually best to give unqualified thanks to the speaker for coming and explaining his views. You can then say that the topic attracts conflicting opinions, and that not everyone will necessarily agree with the speaker. In fact you may want to go further and say that many, or most, people present disagree. However, your thanks should still be sincere and unqualified. Perhaps something like the following might be appropriate.

❻ Dr Wilson deserves our unqualified thanks for so ably explaining the aims of her campaign. Abortion is an issue that arouses very strong feelings and many of us will not have been convinced.

However, there is one thing on which we are unanimous. That is our respect for her courage in coming here, and our appreciation for the tolerant way that she answered our sometimes hostile questions. So please would you join me in a warm round of applause for Dr Wilson. ❾

The comments in this chapter have assumed that the vote of thanks is to a speaker. But of course votes of thanks are frequently given to people who have given their time in some other way, such as musicians, conjurers, or countless others. It makes very little difference to a vote of thanks; it is just that you are thanking a person for what he has done rather than what he has said. You may be praising the musical pitch rather than the humour. The thank you is the same. Here is an example of a short, complete speech.

❻ There are some things that we can do. There are some things that we cannot do, but might if we worked at it for long enough. And there are some things that we could never ever do, even if we practised every day for the rest of our lives. The display of juggling that we have just seen comes firmly in that last category. It was breathtaking.

I want to praise the skill of each member of the Mark Jones Juggling Trio. You came here to entertain us and we have duly been entertained. My word have we been entertained?

We are extremely grateful to you all for giving up an evening, and travelling forty miles for our benefit. It has meant a lot to us. Now it is my privilege to propose a vote of thanks to the Mark Jones Trio. Ladies and gentlemen, please join me in a round of applause. **9**

SUMMARY

1 Thank the performer by name, and get the facts right.
2 Make the speech short.
3 Make the approach warm and sincere.
4 Praise generously but not excessively, especially if the performance was not good.
5 It is fine to prepare in advance, but try and make part of your speech topical to the actual performance. This shows sincerity.
6 End with a climax and perhaps a round of applause.

17

PRESENTATION TO A PERSON LEAVING

These are usually made in a working environment to a person leaving a job. However, presentations are also made in other circumstances, for example to a voluntary worker who is leaving after long service.

There are several types of occasion and they call for subtle differences in approach. Later in this chapter they are considered separately and short specimen speeches are given under each of the following headings:

- Presentation to an employee retiring on reaching normal retirement age.
- Presentation to an employee retiring or leaving due to poor health.
- Presentation to a good employee leaving to take another job.
- Presentation to a problem employee leaving to take another job.
- Presentation to an employee leaving because of redundancy.
- Presentation to a person leaving for family reasons.
- Replies to the presentations.

It is particularly important that the speaker gets the facts right. The beneficiary will know if there is a mistake and may resent it. Others may know as well.

You will probably recall presentations where mistakes were made, and I certainly can. Worst of all was where a director thanked Mary for nine years' loyal service in which she had risen right up to Grade B. He also mentioned her achievement in playing tennis for the county. Everyone knew that she had worked for the company for fourteen years, she was on Grade A, and that her sport was netball.

Part of the motive for making a presentation speech is usually a sincere wish to thank the leaver, and to record his or her achievements. Another part of the motivation will be to nurture the morale of the rest of the group. For both these reasons you should take care to get it right.

In most cases you will want to include at least one personal anecdote. This can be interesting on its own or, even better, it may show how the leaving person has helped the group. There may be room for humour, perhaps mentioning a well known idiosyncrasy.

The presentations are usually made with people standing in a group. A long speech will not be appreciated, and in most cases you will not want to speak for more than two or three minutes. An exception would be if it was at a formal event such as a dinner. In these circumstances a formal speech would be expected and welcomed.

You should try hard to make your speech sincere, though this may not always be easy. You may hold warm feelings about most of your staff and colleagues, but not necessarily all of them. Some leavers are no great loss to the organisation. Try to leave out reference to any bad characteristics, and dwell on the good points that you can praise with sincerity. Everyone has got some of these.

On the other hand you should not go to the other extreme and wildly overpraise the leaving person. This is insincere too. Remember the story of the small boy who accompanied his mother to the graveyard. After reading several of the tombstones he asked her where the sinners were buried.

You will always be mindful of group morale. So it may be appropriate to take group credit for helping the leaving person progress to a higher position. The others may be able to take pride in this and some may feel that it can happen to them as well.

The two principal points of the speech will be to praise and thank the recipient. These should therefore be prominent in your presentation. Remember the two points. **Praise** and **thanks**. You should also remember that the recipient is the reason that the speech is being made and why everyone is gathered together. Do not allow your own part to become too prominent and detract from the other person's glory. Any anecdotes should focus on the other person and if you figure in them your role should only be incidental.

You will probably conclude your speech by handing over an object. Do not fiddle with the object whilst you are speaking as this may be distracting. It is a good idea to produce the present with a flourish at the end of the speech. This can be a very effective climax.

Presentation to an employee on reaching normal retirement age

Specimen speech

- **TIME** *2–2¹/₂ minutes*

❝ This is one of the milestone days of Peter's life. Think about them. There's the day that you are born, your first day at school, the day that you get married. Some of us have more than one of those days, but not Peter, and it's marvellous to see Julia here with him today.

Right there on the list is the day that you retire and for Peter that's today. It's a day for looking back and assessing what you have achieved. For Peter it's quite a lot and he enjoyed doing it.

Not many of us can remember it, but twelve years ago the London region had just two salesmen, and they sold twenty trucks. Now it's twelve salesmen and last year they sold more than two hundred.

Several people helped achieve that, and some of them are here today, but Peter's contribution was vital. He led from the front and he did it with a smile on his face. And the old hands still remember the Simpson contract. Who else but Peter would have made that journey at three in the morning?

Peter, we know that the coming years are going to be exciting and we wish you great happiness in your retirement. On behalf of the whole company I am pleased to present you with this gold watch. ❞

This contains humour – the reference to some people (probably including the speaker) having had more than one wedding day. It should sound sincere, especially the references to the leaver's cheerful character. It praises his achievements and mentions one in particular, the way that he got the Simpson contract. It brings in the rest of the group and it wishes the leaver well in the future. Here is another one along the same lines:

Specimen speech

- **TIME** *2–2¹/₂ minutes*

❢ This is both a time to look back and a time to look forward. There are so many happy times to look back on, and a lot of people have enjoyed working with Jill. I am one of them.

My job has been easier than it might have been. We have had virtually no problems with the purchase ledger, not even last year when we changed the computer system. We have a lot to thank you for, and on behalf of the management I want you to know that we are grateful.

We will do our best without you, but there is just one problem that frightens us. Can we manage to keep twenty-six pot plants going? I fear that you may have put a curse on us. And if just one dies we will be struck down.

I know that Jill is looking forward to retirement with pleasurable anticipation. Both the Girl Guides and the greenhouse are going to get more of her time, and there is a trip to Australia coming up.

Jill, everyone in the company joins me in wishing you well. On behalf of them all, I would like you to accept this as a token of our appreciation. ❢

Presentation to an employee retiring or leaving due to poor health

There must be some sadness about this speech, perhaps only a little or perhaps a great deal. The speaker should not ignore this and should put into words what everyone will be thinking.

Having done this he should be as positive about the future as is realistically possible in the circumstances. He should still, of course, thank the retiring person for their work and achievements, and fulfil the other requirements of a presentation to a retiring person.

The following example can be adjusted according to the seriousness of the illness and the prospects for the future.

Specimen speech

- **TIME** *1¹/₂–2 minutes*

  ❝ We all wish that I could be making this presentation in five years' time. That is because we all wish that Charles could have stayed with us up to the usual retiring age. It is such a shame that ill health is cutting short his career in local government. We are all the losers.

  But let us not be despondent. Let us think of all that Charles has done here in the last eight years. We all have our memories of what he has achieved, but high on everybody's list must be the reorganisation of the licensing section. We will see the benefits for years to come, and so will the public.

  Let us not be despondent about the future either. Charles has extra years to enjoy his retirement and there is so much that he is going to do. It's true that he will not be doing any mountain climbing, but he is a man with so many hobbies, stamp collecting and photography to name just two. And I believe that novel really will be written and published.

  So Charles, here's to the future. Please accept this bowl as a mark of our respect and as an acknowledgement of all that you have done. You take into retirement the best wishes of us all. ❞

– Presentation to a good – employee leaving to take another job

Specimen speech

- **TIME** *1¹/₂–2 minutes*

  ❝ This is getting boring. It's the third time this year that I have made a presentation to someone being promoted to a position in head office. Once again Plymouth's loss is head office's gain.

  I just do not know how they would manage without us. Still the well has not run dry yet. Abdul is taking over Susan's job on Monday, and I reckon I could be making yet another speech in six months' time.

But back to the point, and Susan you are the point. You have not been here very long but you have done a smashing job for us, especially in getting the dormant accounts tidied up. Thank you for your work, and especially for the last six months when you were supervisor. And congratulations on the promotion. It really is deserved.

And please, when you get to London, do try to make them cut down on all those memos that they send us.

So Susan, all the best, and I am pleased to give this to you from all your friends in Plymouth. 〙

This speech contains humour which is very suitable for a speech acknowledging an internal promotion (the reference to the proceedings getting boring and the digs at head office). A joke at the expense of head office will be well received in most organisations, except in head office of course!

It fortifies team spirit by emphasising that the Plymouth office is special, and by mentioning that several people have done well and that great things are expected of the next person in the job. It also fulfils the function of thanking the leaver and wishing her well in the future.

The next speech is intended for a popular and valuable employee who is leaving to take a job with a competitor. It too contains humour, and endeavours to foster team spirit.

Specimen speech

● **TIME** *1¹/₂–2 minutes*

〘 I have mixed feelings in saying goodbye to Richard. You know the definition of mixed feelings. It's what you have when your mother-in-law drives your new car over a cliff.

My feelings are sad because I am sorry to see Richard go, especially as he will be working for one of our competitors. On the other hand, it is a well-deserved promotion. And on the positive side I will no longer feel jealous every time I see that flash car in the car park.

So let us wish him well and thank him for all that he has done for us. I am very grateful, especially for the way that he sorted out the servicing backlog.

I hope that he does well for his new employer. They could do with a bit of help. We are not afraid of healthy competition and I say let the best team win. Sorry about that Richard.

Seriously though! All the best. And please accept this from all your friends here. ❞

— Presentation to a problem — employee leaving to take another job

This is, of course, a particularly difficult speech to make. You may decide to ignore the problem aspect, and just make a standard speech as you would to any other leaver. This is understandable, but if you do take this line you should be careful not to sound insincere, and also you should be careful with any humour that is used.

The recipient, and probably the rest of the group, will be aware of the problem. They will be sensitive to any atmosphere, and will be watching how you handle the situation. Do not say anything insincere, and limit praise to the truth.

There is something to be said for bringing a problem into the open. Here is an example of how it might be done.

Specimen speech

● **TIME** *2–2¹/₂ minutes*

❞ It is not a very well-kept secret that Bill and the directors have not seen eye to eye on everything. In fact, it would be more accurate to say that he thinks that one aspect of the recent changes is a bad mistake. We have not seen it that way and we still don't.

So it is the well-known problem of the irresistible force and the immovable object. And in the circumstances Bill feels that his future lies elsewhere. It's a shame, but I respect his courage and I respect the decision that he has made. I know that everyone feels the same and wishes him all the luck in the world in his new career. Despite the present difference of view we have been through a lot together. The company has a lot to thank Bill for and it is not forgotten. The transport department is in fine shape, and in particular Bill has done a first-rate job in extending the life of the fleet. Thank you!

Now Bill, you are not going to leave without taking a token of our best wishes with you. Every single member of staff has signed this card, and we would like you to accept this clock from the company. All the best, and please keep in touch. **9**

Presentation to an employee leaving because of redundancy

This too is a difficult speech to make. The fact of the redundancy can hardly be ignored, so it must be acknowledged in the speech. Needless to say, you should say that you are sorry that the redundancy has happened, and it is probably wise to say that no blame attaches to the person leaving. Here is an example of how it can be done.

Specimen speech

● **TIME** *1¹/₂–2 minutes*

6 I have made quite a few presentation speeches and they have nearly all been happy affairs. We have been saying goodbye to someone who is leaving because they have chosen to do so, and usually because they are moving on to greater things. As we all know, today is not like that.

The reason is well known, but I will say it again. The loss of the government contract means that there is just not as much work in the packing department.

We have to make a cut of two people and we are doing it on the basis of last in first out. Pauline has been here for just eleven months, and that is why she is one of the two people going.

I could not have asked for more commitment, and it's such a shame that it has had to happen this way.

Pauline, in the short time that you have been here you have made a lot of friends. And we are very sorry that you are leaving.

I know that you have two interviews lined up for next week and we wish you success with them. Whoever takes you on will be doing themselves a favour.

All the best Pauline, and please accept this with the warmest wishes of us all. **9**

Presentation to an employee leaving for family reasons

These are nearly always very happy occasions, though an exception may be someone leaving to look after a sick or elderly relative. Happy occasions include a presentation to someone leaving to get married or to have a baby. Presentations to these leavers are normally joyful, light-hearted affairs, and best wishes for the marriage or baby play an important part.

The following is an example of a presentation speech for someone leaving to have a baby.

Specimen speech

● **TIME** *1¹/₂–2 minutes*

6 Presentations are sometimes sad affairs, but there could not be a more cheerful occasion than this. There are not many good reasons for leaving us, but starting a family has to be one of them.

We are absolutely delighted for you Gwen, and we wish John and yourself every happiness in your new role as parents.

We have enjoyed having you here in the last three years, and we have come to depend on the way that you organise the front office. We will all miss you for a lot of reasons, but I will especially. No one else can read my writing!

It would be nice to think that you will be coming back in a few months' time, but we respect your decision to be a full-time mother. Perhaps in years to come? Let's hope so.

So Gwen, thank you for all that you have done for us. This present is on behalf of us all. And we look forward to you bringing the baby to see us next March. **9**

—— **Replies to the presentation** ——

A good reply should have many of the features of a good presentation speech. It should nearly always be short, good-natured, light-hearted and if possible with a touch of humour.

You should strive to say nice things about your colleagues and the organisation that you are leaving. Hopefully this will come easily to you, but just possibly it will not. You should in any case be kind, right up to the limits of sincerity. Here is an example:

Specimen speech

● **TIME** *2–2¹/₂ minutes*

6 I had no idea that this was planned and I am completely at a loss for words. I have nothing prepared and I just do not know what to say.

(TAKE LARGE SHEAF OF NOTES FROM POCKET – [LAUGHTER])

Sincerely though, I do thank you for your very kind words and this marvellous gift of a new fishing rod. It's quite the best that I have ever owned and it's bound to improve my results no end. With my old rod I sometimes nearly caught fish ten inches long. With this one I will nearly be able to catch fish twelve inches long.

Be that as it may, I will use it most weekends, and I shall think of you all every time that I do. Just think of that. Every Saturday morning at twelve o'clock you will be cashing up, and I will be fishing with this rod and thinking about you. It will be nice for us all.

And talking of work, I have enjoyed the years that I have been here, and I have enjoyed working with you all. I am looking forward to my new job but I would not change a single day of the last six years.

Once again, thank you for this magnificent present. I could not have chosen anything that I like better. I will keep in touch and I look forward to seeing you soon. **9**

SUMMARY

1 There are different types of occasion. They call for slightly different types of speech.
2 Get the facts right.
3 Personal anecdotes are particularly suitable, especially humorous ones.
4 Unless there is a special event such as a dinner, the speech should be short.
5 The two main points should usually be praise and thanks.
6 Try and speak with sincerity.
7 Remember that the recipient is the main character, not yourself.

18

CLUB OFFICERS' REPORTS

The term 'club' encompasses hundreds of thousands of different bodies. Some of these are based on hobbies such as gardening and stamp collecting, likely to be known by the grand names of horticulture and philately. Then there are clubs whose members practise public speaking (Toastmasters and the Association of Speakers Clubs). The term also covers sports clubs, many charities, political pressure groups, and so on. Some clubs may be affiliated to a large organisation, in the way that individual football clubs are affiliated to the Football Association.

The members of most clubs delegate the day-to-day running to a committee. The composition of the committee varies according to the club and its purpose, but common to most is a chairman, a secretary and a treasurer. The committee members report to the full membership at an annual general meeting (AGM), and sometimes more frequently.

Almost everyone is a member of one or more clubs, so you will be familiar with the system of club officers reporting to members. It is highly likely that you will have seen it done badly, and that you will have sat through many reports that waste everyone's time. Some of the common failings are:

- The speaker delivers the report in a boring and tedious manner. Reports are frequently read, which is potentially the most boring style of delivery. Unfortunately some speakers drone on in a flat voice, avoiding gestures and eye contact, and generally sending everyone to sleep.

- The speaker makes the report too long. AGMs are usually grouped with some other activity, such as a guest speaker. If it is a table tennis club, for example, the members usually want to get the meeting over so that they can play table tennis.
- The report consists of lists. The information given may be useful, and even necessary, but lists are usually a way of losing audience attention.
- A report duplicates information given in other reports in the same meeting. This may not be entirely the officer's fault. It is not unknown for a Chairman to commence with a comprehensive report covering every aspect of the club's activities. Following reports are then likely to duplicate what has already been said, and some events may be included in three or four other reports.
- A report may state the obvious. For example a cricket captain may report that only one match was won in the whole season. It is very unlikely that the audience would be unaware of this fact. It is like the constitutional American requirement that State Governors be informed of the death of a President. All State Governors knew of President Kennedy's assassination within a few minutes of the event, but they were still informed by letter some days later.
- A report may convey trivial information. Even if it is well put the members can survive, and even thrive, without the information.
- Unfortunately, a report may be used to further personal feuds and settle grievances. The message of the report may be 'I told you so'.

The following points suggest ways of avoiding these common failings:

- Remember that a boring delivery is the enemy of all speech making, including reports. Keep eye contact with the audience, do not speak in a monotone, and study Chapter 6 of this book.
- As with all speeches, be hard on yourself concerning time.
- Try to avoid lists, and if you do have them, keep them short. In *The Mikado*, the Lord High Executioner had a little list and it was very amusing, but most lists are not.
- Only include information relevant to your function. If you are the Treasurer, report the finances, not whether the pitch needs cutting more often. It may be worth speaking to other committee members in advance. This way you can make sure that you do not duplicate each other.
- Be sparing in reporting the obvious. If this means that your report is short, so much the better.
- Do not burden the audience with the trivial.
- Leave politics to the politicians.

You must be mindful of the constitution of the club, and if it is a member of a wider organisation you must be mindful of that as well. For example, certain churches require statistics to be kept concerning church attendance. These must be kept and reported.

If a lot of detail is essential it is worth considering a written report. Your verbal report can highlight the key points with the detail available for inspection separately. To return to the point about church attendance, the written report could list the figures for each week individually. In the verbal report you might just say that attendances averaged 83 and that this was six more than last year. A written report that incorporates the accounts is suitable for a treasurer. The accounts should be distributed, the treasurer should spotlight one or two key facts and trends, and then he should make himself available for questions.

You may want to use the report to convey a particular message or theme. An audience is usually able to assimilate a few key points and it may be important that they concentrate on certain important developments. Examples could be a decline in membership or a need for extra revenue.

A chairman might use his report to convey certain praise and thanks. This will probably be to his fellow committee members, and perhaps to other key people and to the members generally. Other committee members may want to thank and praise also. For example, a treasurer may want to thank the membership for paying subscriptions on time. Complaints may be in order if cooperation has not been forthcoming, but this should be worded with care.

Finally, we turn to things that need to be done in the future. The report is an opportunity to spell out forthcoming challenges, and work that needs to be done. It is also an opportunity to warn of problems that lie ahead, and of consequences to be faced if things are not done. Perhaps it is a time to be inspirational and to try to motivate club members.

The following is an example of a chairman's report to the members of a photographic club. It has been a good year and he has been supported by an enthusiastic committee and membership. The chairman, who is retiring, wants to report in detail, deliver his thanks, and challenge the members to do even better. The club has financial problems.

Chairman's report to the members of a photographic club

- **TIME** *3¹/₂–4 minutes*

❝ I am pleased to present my report on what has been, in the main, a very satisfactory year. We have had a full programme of ten educational meetings. Eight of these were successful and well supported, and the lecture by Professor Jones was outstanding. Two of our meetings were less successful and your committee has fully considered the reasons for this.

Next year's programme was published last week and I trust that you will agree that it is a full and lively list. I particularly draw your attention to the longer Christmas break and an extra meeting in November. We are making this change at the clear wish of most members, who felt that December was overloaded. One of our two flops last year was just before Christmas.

Once again our competitions attracted a very high standard of entrants. We had several very worthy winners, and in particular congratulations are due to Bernard Quinn who won the Goldberg Cup for the fourth time.

Although it has been a good year there is one cloud in the sky, and I am referring to the club's financial position. This will be explained by the Treasurer shortly, but I do want to emphasise the seriousness of the problem and the need for some tough and realistic decisions.

This is my last report to you as Chairman and despite the financial problems I am reporting on a strong club. I am giving up the office after three years, and in doing so I would like to pay tribute to my fellow officers. They have given me magnificent support. And I would also like to thank you, the members, for your help and encouragement. I have enjoyed every minute of it.

We have achieved nearly all our aims in the last three years, but one has eluded us – the one hundredth member. We peaked at ninety-four last year and membership stands at ninety-one today.

Wouldn't it be a fantastic achievement to have one hundred members in our club? All that we do, and a hundred members as well.

There are two hundred thousand people living in this city, so recruiting nine of them should not be impossible. This is my parting challenge to you. Make this a club with one hundred members. I shall be back here next year to shake the Chairman's hand if he's done it. **9**

SUMMARY

1 Many reports are very boring. Read Chapter 6 of this book and make yours one of the exceptions.
2 Keep it short and consider a written report (especially treasurers).
3 Try not to duplicate the reports of others. Complain privately afterwards if anyone does it to you.
4 Do not be trivial.
5 Avoid politics and personal grudges.
6 Keep in mind any particular requirements of the club constitution.

19

TO THANK A PERSON OR GROUP FOR HARD WORK AND ACHIEVEMENT

A speech to say thank you is often neglected, and when it is done it is often not done as well as its subject deserves. Nearly all readers will recognise the truth of this statement, and many will instinctively think of occasions when they themselves did not receive the thanks and recognition that were due. This is important, most obviously in the business world, but also in thousands of voluntary bodies and other organisations. Other chapters in this book have touched on the delivery of a proper thank you.

Speeches of thanks vary a lot but these are some of the key points to watch:

- Try to make your speech as sincere as possible. The human race has a great talent for spotting insincerity. As you will be preparing the speech this should not be too difficult, but if it is absolutely impossible you should perhaps consider if someone else should do the speech.
  The talent to spot insincerity was once well expressed by a great lawyer, commenting on the jury system. He said that juries frequently give the right verdict for the wrong reasons. They often fail to follow the evidence and the legal points. Instead they look at the accused, and at the witnesses, and ask themselves who they believe to be sincere. Their verdict is given accordingly, and it is the same one that they would have given by following the evidence and the legal points.
- Thank people by name. If you are thanking just one person the name is obvious. If you are thanking a group consider mentioning

all the names (if it is a small group), or some of the names (if it is a large group). People do appreciate hearing their name.

There are two traps to avoid. Do not mention so many names that the speech becomes a list. This is dull and it may devalue the names most worthy of mention. Also, make sure that you mention the key people. They will know who they are and the audience probably will too. So make sure that you get it right.

- Do not overpraise. Give praise where it is due. Possibly give slightly more praise than is strictly due. But do not go farther than that. Too much praise is insincere and may be counterproductive. It will probably sound patronising and the recipients will know that it is not entirely deserved.

- Try to make the speech sound spontaneous. It will probably, and quite rightly, be well prepared, but nevertheless try and make it sound as spontaneous as possible. The early chapters of this book gave advice on this, particularly Chapter 6 on the subject of delivery. Maybe you can add something heard at the very last minute, or a reply to a comment just made. Remember Mark Twain who said that an awful lot of work went into preparing his spontaneous speeches.

- Try and make the speech personal. The audience may appreciate a formula speech, but they will appreciate more a speech that has obviously been prepared especially for them. For example, a formula speech may be given by the chairman of a national charity. He or she may go round the country thanking groups for their fund–raising efforts. Virtually the same speech could probably be used each time, but it would be a formula speech.

  It would be better to quote individual names and individual anecdotes relating to a particular section. It is better to show how much money has been raised locally and how part of it will be spent locally. This is a tall order, so perhaps the core of a standard speech could be heavily adapted to suit individual localities and circumstances.

- It is useful to say what the results of the efforts that you are praising have been. The listeners may not know exactly, or even if they do know they may well like to hear it spelt out. For example:

❦ The result of this great effort was that the small town of Witney contributed £6000 to the national fund. Well done! ❧

   or

❦ During the month of October we monitored customer

complaints. They fell by 30 per cent compared with the first nine months of the year. That is a splendid achievement and it is due to your efforts. Thank you! **9**

- People should be thanked often, but not too often. A speech of thanks delivered too frequently loses its impact.
- Do not forget the contribution of the back room staff. Sometimes it is only the people doing the high profile tasks who get noticed and thanked. This can apply to sales staff who bring back the orders, but who may be supported by secretaries, estimators, and a host of others. The people with a lower profile appreciate thanks as well, and frequently deserve it.
- There is usually a strong correlation between hard work and achievement. But one does not always follow from the other. It is possible to praise the effort and thank people for trying, even if the results have been disappointing. Indeed, a speech in these circumstances may be particularly needed and appreciated.
- It may be a good idea to include some points of detail in your speech. This will show that you noticed their particular effort and cared about it.
- It is appreciated when the top person shares the credit. This can be along the lines of 'It was a team effort. I could not have done it without your help. Thank you.'
- It can be very effective to be brutally frank and foster a spirit of 'all in this together'. Earl Mountbatten did this in a speech when he said that many of his soldiers felt that they were the forgotten army. He continued by saying that it was not true that people had forgotten them. This was because people never knew that they existed.

These principles are shown in the following short specimen speeches. The first is to thank the committee of a voluntary organisation.

Specimen speech to thank the committee of a youth club

- **TIME** *2¹/₂–3 minutes*

  6 The seven people on this committee represent an awful lot. For a start they represent fourteen hundred hours' hard work in the last year. That's right. You can check if you like. Four hours a week each on average.

They represent an awful lot of wisdom and experience. What a combination. A bank manager, a farmer, two retired school teachers, a nurse, a minister of religion, and the owner of our local dispensing chemist.

I do not list them in any particular order. The fact that I mentioned the bank manager first has no connection at all with the fact that my overdraft is due for renewal, and I am seeing him on Tuesday. Please be kind to me Bill.

They represent a great spirit and an unfailing cheerfulness. We have all felt the benefit and I have special reason to thank them for it. Their support and encouragement helped me to give my best. I could not have done it without them.

And what has been their reward for all of this? In one sense absolutely nothing. Not a penny in salary, and a level of expenses that does not really cover what they put in.

But on every other count the rewards are very considerable. You have the reward of knowing that you have done a good job. You have the reward of knowing that parents and others are grateful. You know that I am grateful. Above all you have the reward of watching thirty-four teenagers benefit from what you do.

Bill, Alice, Charlie, Susan, Mohammed, Pauline, Barbara, I thank you all. One day they will get round to making a film about you. And when they do I shall suggest that they call it *The Magnificent Seven*. Thank you for all that you have done. **9**

This short speech contains a lot of (presumably) sincere praise and it names each member of the committee. It mentions three times in succession the phrase 'they represent' which is an effective technique. It praises the committee members' high principles in working with no monetary reward, and it assures them that a lot of people are very grateful.

The speech contains two good jokes. The film title *The Magnificent Seven* can only be used if there are seven people being thanked. However, you may be able to adapt the idea to some other number. *The Dirty Dozen* comes to mind and also Enid Blyton's *Famous Five*. The joke about meeting the bank manager to renew the overdraft may be adapted to some other profession. A visit to a doctor or dentist for some treatment is one possibility.

The second specimen speech illustrates thanks to a fund-raising committee.

Specimen speech to thank the hard work and success of a group that has raised £100,000

- **TIME** *3–3¹/₂ minutes*

❦ There are a lot of people who would like to thank you this afternoon. One or two are here with me, but there are many more who are grateful for what you have done.

Our retirement home in Cambridge faces constant anxiety about funds. The work that you have done has gone a long way towards easing that anxiety, and securing its future. Everyone at St Margarets, the residents, the staff, the Board of Managers, recognises this and thanks you for it. They would all like to thank you in person, but it is my privilege to speak for them all.

The sum that you raised was £100,000. It's an incredible amount and it took a tremendous amount of work. There were the special events, the sponsored cycle ride, the coffee mornings, and most especially I remember the house-to-house collections last February. It was the wettest week of the year, but you were out every night.

All that did not just happen, it was made to happen. It took a lot of hard work and it took a lot of clever ideas. Some of these were very original. Everyone has coffee mornings, but it takes genius to persuade the local superstore to donate the coffee – and get them to give a £500 donation as well – and talk the local newspaper into photographing the manager handing it over. Dick! I know that was your idea. Well done!

You have earned the right to sit back and have a rest now, but I was thrilled to hear that you are going to extend your efforts into next year. Perhaps I could humbly use the words in the book of common prayer 'In thanks for mercies past received and in hope of mercies still to come'.

Joan, Peter, Celia, Stephen, Rosemary and all of you. On behalf of everyone at St Margarets, thank you and well done. ❧

This speech mentions the names, hopefully those that should particularly be mentioned. The reference to the donation of the coffee adds sparkle to the speech, and shows that the speaker has shown a personal interest.

SUMMARY

1 Sincerity is very important. Be sincere and let it show.
2 Mention names but avoid lists of names. Make sure that you mention the key people.
3 Avoid a formula speech of thanks. Put in personal stories and perhaps add something at the last moment.
4 Say what the hard work has achieved.
5 Share the credit.
6 Do not forget the hard workers in the background.

20

AN ADDRESS AT A FUNERAL OR MEMORIAL SERVICE

A funeral or memorial service will almost always include a few personal words from the minister of religion conducting it. Often, but not always, there will be one or more addresses as well. In my experience they are almost always extremely well done, moving, and much appreciated by the family and friends of the deceased.

It is understandable that you should feel concern if asked to deliver such an address. It is likely that you are being asked partly because you are a member of the family, or a close friend of the deceased. In these circumstances you will wonder how you will cope with your own grief. You will also be anxious that you do not let down the family and the memory of the dead person. After all there is only one funeral service and usually only one memorial service. You will not have a second chance.

Grief and emotion are not a bar to delivering a suitable address. Indeed, many moving and appreciated tributes are delivered in the face of these feelings. They may be the extra factors that make an address memorable. Obviously, this is only true up to a point. If you really cannot do the job without breaking down it is best to decline.

Most speakers take the view that the feelings of the family are paramount. So in planning the address, ask yourself what they would like you to say. If you are not sure, it might be a good idea to ask.

You will probably want to make the address relatively short. About three or four minutes is often suitable. Very obviously, only positive things should be said. Have very firmly in your mind that the point of the address is to honour the dead person. Do not put yourself forward in the address. If you do so it should only be to illustrate a point about the deceased, not to make a point about yourself.

It is common for an address to include a quotation from the Bible or from another religious book. If the deceased or the family had a favourite piece of scripture this may well be included. Not everyone will agree, but the magnificent and traditional language of the authorised version is very often preferred. The following pieces of scripture are often used, and often give great comfort.

❛ *To everything there is a season, and a time to every purpose under the heaven:*

A time to be born, and a time to die; a time to plant, and a time to pluck up that which is planted;

A time to kill, and a time to heal; a time to break down, and a time to build up;

A time to weep, and a time to laugh; a time to mourn, and a time to dance. ❜ Ecclesiastes 3:1–4

❛ *The Lord is my shepherd; I shall not want.*

He maketh me to lie down in green pastures: he leadeth me beside the still waters.

He restoreth my soul: he leadeth me in the paths of righteousness for his name's sake.

Yea, though I walk through the valley of the shadow of death, I will fear no evil: for thou art with me; thy rod and thy staff they comfort me.

Thou preparest a table before me in the presence of mine enemies: thou anointest my head with oil; my cup runneth over.

Surely goodness and mercy shall follow me all the days of my life: and I will dwell in the house of the Lord forever. ❜

Psalm 23

The following is not from the Bible and is often quoted for its comfort and reassurance.

❛ *Death is nothing at all. I have only slipped away into the next room. I am I, and you are you. Whatever we were to each other, that we still are. Call me by my old familiar name, speak to me in the easy way which you always used. Put no difference in your tone, wear no forced air of solemnity or sorrow. Laugh as we always laughed at the little jokes we enjoyed together. Let my name be ever the household word that it always was, let it be*

spoken without effort, without the trace of a shadow on it. Life means all that it ever meant. It is the same as it ever was; there is unbroken continuity. Why should I be out of mind because I am out of sight? I am waiting for you, for an interval, somewhere very near, just round the corner.
All is well. 🟡

Henry Scott Holland (1847–1918)
Canon of St. Paul's Cathedral

The address will be a tribute to the dead person and you will be striving to convey the essence of that person's character and achievements. Very often a true story can do this and it may even be humorous. By chance, I have recently attended two funeral services at which a true , humorous story was included in an address.

At the first, the address was given by the dead man's brother-in-law; the brother of his widow. He told of the extremely favourable impression that had been made on the family the first time that the dead man had been brought home. In fact he had quickly told his sister that if she did not marry him, he would marry him himself.

At the second, the address was given by a lady to whose family the dead man had been very kind. Her mother had died when she was a child, leaving the father to care for four children. The dead man had kindly lent her father his car to take them on holiday. Unfortunately her father had written off the car in an accident.

Uncle Frank, as the dead man was affectionately known, had not complained and had lent them his new car the following year. Her father had written off this one too. Uncle Frank still did not complain but brought another car and offered to lend it to them the next year. They would have taken it but the insurance company gave cover for any driver – except Mr R Wood (the lady's father).

On both occasions the stories were told in an emotional way. The response in each case was smiles, just a little laughter and a definite feeling of 'Yes, that was the man we knew.'

Following are two specimen funeral addresses. The first assumes that the deceased, the family, and the speaker have strong religious convictions. The second address does not focus on religion at all. Obviously, the personal details are made up, but the structure and ideas are indicated.

Specimen funeral address

- **TIME** *2¹/₂ – 3 minutes*

  ❛ I would like to say a few words about my friend Frank Turner. Most of us here today knew Frank as a good friend. A few of you knew him through the business but you were undoubtedly friends as well.

  And of course some of you knew Frank as a member of the family. He was a wonderful husband and father, and we all feel for Jane and Peter in their sorrow.

  I knew Frank as a sincere Christian and a regular worshipper at this church. He has gone to meet his maker in the sure and certain hope of everlasting life. This knowledge will be a great comfort to the family and all who grieve.

  I would like to quote the scriptures and I have chosen a much loved piece from the third chapter of John's Gospel. It was a favourite of Frank and it conveys his certainty of heaven.

  For God so loved the world, that he gave his only begotten Son, that whosoever believeth in him should not perish but have everlasting life
  For God sent not his Son into the world to condemn the world: but that the world through him might be saved
  He that believeth in him is not condemned.   John 3:16–18

  Frank's christianity was very much of the practical variety and he lived his faith every day. Most of us have personal memories of his kindness. I certainly have. The work for the Over 60s was just one example, and we all remember all those coach trips that he arranged. And he even drove all the way back to Brighton once when someone was left behind.

  Frank Turner – a great man. We will miss him. ❜

Specimen funeral address

- **TIME** *2¹/₂ – 3 minutes*

  ❛ Saying a few words at a funeral service is a great responsibility, even more so when the funeral is of Julia Matthews. This is because Julia was such an exceptional person. She deserves an exceptional tribute and a rare standard of eloquence.

I am not sure that I can deliver, but I will try. I can certainly say that she was one of the most loved people in this village. I can certainly say that she enriched the life of the village, and that she gave a lot of her time to the service of the village and its people. I can certainly say that she was the world's most popular aunty, both for real nephews and nieces, and for honorary nephews and nieces. The garden at Rose Cottage was always full of children. She positively welcomed balls coming over the hedge into her garden. It meant that a youngster would be along a minute or two later.

My problem is not what to say. It is what to leave out. I will include just one more thing. On Sir Christopher Wren's tomb it says 'If you seek my memorial, look around you'. If you seek Julia's memorial, look around you the next time you go into the Village Hall. The chairs, the kitchen, and next week's production of *The Desert Song*. Julia had a big part in all of that.

I would like to conclude by offering the sympathy of all of us to Julia's sisters and the rest of her family.

She will be missed. 〕

A problem with the two specimen funeral addresses is that they describe fictitious people. You will be describing a very real person. You may choose to concentrate on the structure of the addresses, perhaps borrow the odd phrase, and put in details relevant to the person who you are describing.

SUMMARY

1 Grief and emotion are not a bar to delivering an address. But if you really cannot do it, say no.
2 Controlled grief and emotion may add impact your words.
3 Remember that the objective is to honour the dead person.
4 Remember that the secondary objective is to offer comfort to family and friends.
5 An appropriate reading or quotation can add great weight to your words. Consider the Bible or other religious work, a poem or a favourite book.
6 Try and sum up the best parts of the dead person's character and achievements.
7 An anecdote may well illustrate the character beautifully.

21

EFFECTIVENESS
IN DEBATES

Debating societies exist in many schools, colleges and universities. A few are very well known, such as the Oxford Union. Many leading British politicians developed their skills there, or at its sister body in Cambridge. They also exist outside educational establishments, and are available to adults as well as to students.

Some debates are attended because the participants really care about the subject being debated. They attach significance to the result of the vote and wish to influence that result. A very well-known example is the Oxford Union debate in the 1930s that passed the motion 'This House Would Not Fight For King And Country'. Adolf Hitler was said to have noted the result. Former students of a certain age will probably recall passionate debates about the war in Vietnam and the Campaign For Nuclear Disarmament.

At other debates the participants are involved in an intellectual exercise, just with the aim of doing well. Motions may be topical or they may have such titles as 'This House Believes Enough Is Enough'.

It is usual for a vote to be taken at the end of the debate. This is normally cast on the merits of the motion, but sometimes the audience is asked to vote on the performance of the speakers.

The precise format may differ from debate to debate but typically it will run like this:

- Main Speaker For The Motion   10 minutes
- Main Speaker Against The Motion   10 minutes
- Seconder For The Motion   5 minutes

- Seconder Against The Motion   5 minutes
- Speakers From The Floor
- Summing Up By The Main Speaker Against
  The Motion   5 minutes
- Summing Up By The Main Speaker For
  The Motion   5 minutes

The person proposing the motion always speaks last. This means that the same person speaks first of all and last of all, which is probably an advantage.

The chairman of the debate should strive to be both fair and efficient, so if you are taking this role keep the following in mind:

- You must be scrupulously fair and not favour one side. Do not let your personal views interfere with this fairness.
- Commence the debate by reading the exact wording of the motion. The exact wording can be important. For example, a debate about monarchy may be a general motion about monarchy in the abstract. Or it may be specifically about the British Monarch.
- Before introducing the first speaker, summarise the main rules, conventions and time limitations. Introduce the timekeeper and show how any warning lights work.
- You should hold the speakers to the time limits. But, if you stretch a point for one speaker you should do the same for the others.
- Endeavour to call speakers from the floor according to an assessment of the flow of the debate. This means if you believe that six are likely to favour the motion and six oppose it, and there is only time for eight speakers, you should call four from each camp.
- There may be a fine line between good-natured banter and unpleasant abuse. It is your job to see that the line is not crossed. In an extreme case you may have to stop someone speaking. You may need to request participants to behave in a courteous manner.
- At the end of the debate you should call for the vote. You may count it yourself or appoint tellers to do the counting. You do not vote yourself. You announce the result in the following manner 'Votes in favour 74. Votes against 93. I declare that the motion is lost'. If the votes are tied you exercise your casting vote.
- Most debates are held at least partly for pleasure. Keep this in mind and preside in a friendly and good-natured way.

We now move on to speaking in a debate. There are four types of speeches and we will consider them in turn:

- The two main speeches.
- The seconders' speeches.
- Speeches from the floor.
- The two summing up speeches.

It is obviously important that the main speaker and seconder operate as a team. They should discuss the outline of their speeches in advance. This is to prevent them making the same points, which seems to happen surprisingly often. The seconder should complement the main speaker by putting forward different arguments, or by filling in detail on the points already raised. He or she should not be a carbon-copy of the main speaker, or appear to contradict him.

When the debate is in progress they may help each other by passing notes. In particular, information may be made available to help the person summing up at the end. This can take the form of a key fact or outline ideas. These notes should be extremely simple, brief, and in large lettering. A person preparing notes for summing up is working under stress and is not helped by a mass of detailed material. Something like this is ideal.

WRONG – MARGARET THATCHER WENT TO A GRAMMAR SCHOOL

A successful debater thinks on his or her feet and is adept at answering points raised by the opposition. However, do not make the mistake of spending so much time countering the opposition that you neglect to make your own case. Debaters frequently fall into this trap. The risk is of course greater for the side opposing the motion, because the proposing side has one main speech with no points having been made in advance.

———————— **The main speech** ————————

A main speech should set out the principal case for or against the motion. It is a special type of speech but all the main points of speech making are still important. These were explained in the first section of this book and it is well worth referring back to it.

The speech should be a mixture of logic and emotion. The phrase 'logic on fire' sums up what you are trying to achieve. Try to make this speech memorable, try to make it sparkle, and use the techniques explained earlier in this book. Sound construction is very important with a speech of this type and, needless to say, the speech should be persuasive.

All this is best illustrated with an example of a powerful, logical and persuasive speech, proposing a topical political motion.

Specimen speech proposing the motion 'This House Believes That Britain Should Withdraw From The European Union'

● **TIME** *6 – 7 minutes*

❛ My grandfather was killed in the First World War. Last night I had a moving dream. I dreamt that I was transported back in time and spoke to him just before he died.

I told him about life in Britain today, the good things and the bad things. I told him that in some ways parliament was no longer free to make our own laws. Compulsory seat belts for coaches is one example. And I told him that in some areas British courts no longer had the final say in interpreting the law. They could be overruled by a European court.

My grandfather looked sad. 'So we lost the war?' he said. I told him that, on the contrary, we had been victorious. 'So there was a second war, and we lost that one?' he asked. I told him that there had indeed been a second war, but that we had been victorious again. His third question was 'Well then, why?'

I told my grandfather that we had voluntarily surrendered parliament's supreme authority to make laws. And we had voluntarily surrendered the supreme authority of the British courts. To make matters worse, we might be about to surrender our own currency and our right to levy our own taxes.

Grandfather could not understand it. Ladies and gentlemen, I do not understand it. Surely, you do not understand it. Fortunately there is still a chance to reverse it, which is why I ask you to support the motion.

Nothing is worth the loss of our sovereignty. Too much of that sovereignty has gone, and more will go soon.

You are all aware of hundreds of pettifogging examples. We

groan under health and safety regulations that we do not want or need. Business people spend countless hours satisfying European bureaucrats. The word INTRASTAT reduces strong people to quivering jelly. Many of you are smiling. You know what I mean.

I say all this in no spirit of hostility to our European friends. I like them. I like their countries. And when I visit them I expect to observe their laws and customs. Why then should they tell us what to do within our frontiers?

Why did we do it? Of course I do know the reason. We did it because we thought that there were trading advantages, and because we did not believe that the rest would really happen. But it did.

The price would have been too high even if we had got all the trading advantages. But the truth is that these were illusory. Just look at the countries that voted to stay out. Look at Switzerland. Look at Norway. Are they suffering? Quite the contrary, despite all the warnings given to them. They are doing better than we are. Is it impossible to buy Japanese goods in the shops of Britain? Being outside the European Union has not harmed Japan.

European countries would still trade with us. They would do it because it is in their own interests. The Germans would still want to sell us their Mercedes cars. The French would still want to sell us their Camembert cheese. And both would still want to buy our Scotch Whisky and our other goods. They would buy them just as they buy Japanese goods. And we would be able to build up our trade with Australia, America, and especially the Pacific Rim countries of Asia. That is most important of all. The area of the future.

I am not asking you to choose between principle and self-interest. Happily, principle and self-interest are on the same side of the argument. A vote for the motion is a vote for Britain's future prosperity. And it is a vote for Britain's future self-government.

Ladies and gentlemen! I propose the motion and ask for your support. **9**

The opening part of the speech is an emotional appeal to the British people's feelings about sovereignty. The idea of a conversation with a soldier killed in the First World War is taken from an article by Alan Clark.

The speech is a mixture of ideas, facts with concrete examples, and an appeal to self-interest. The inability of parliament to make a fully independent law on the subject of seat belts on coaches is a concrete example.

The speech lends itself to emphasis in certain places. Examples are 'Well then, **why**?' and 'Nothing is worth the loss of our sovereignty'.

It is always good to pick up on audience reaction. Any business person in the audience is likely to smile or nod at the mention of INTRASTAT.

——— The seconder's speech ———

The seconder's speech will probably counter some of the points made by the opposing main speaker, and it will further argue the case for the motion. This may be with new arguments or it may develop arguments made by the proposer. Here is an example of a speech seconding the same motion. It assumes that the main speaker opposing has made dire warnings that the other members would be outraged by British withdrawal, and would make things very difficult.

Specimen speech seconding the motion 'This House Believes That Britain Should Withdraw From The European Union'

- **TIME** *2¹/₂–3 minutes*

   ❛ You have just heard a lot of alarmist nonsense about what the other countries will do when we withdraw. In fact they will not mind at all. They might even be rather pleased. We disagree on so many things that they will probably be relieved. They will be free to develop the European Union as they want, without us making difficulties.

We will depart as friends. And just as we negotiated the terms to go in, we will negotiate the terms to come out. That is in their interests just as much as it is in ours. And please note that the motion says that we should withdraw. It does not say that we should withdraw tomorrow.

My colleague touched on the trading advantages that Britain would enjoy by coming out. I would like to explain these in more detail.

Free trade is a wonderful thing. It was Britain's policy when we were most successful, and it is the policy of the most successful countries now. The European Union stands for the opposite of free trade. There is supposed to be free trade between the member countries, but even that is debatable. How free is the competition between British Airways and the massively subsidised Air France?

But there are trading barriers against the rest of the world. If we cut ourselves free we will improve our trade with our friends in America, in Australia, and elsewhere. And we will be more closely associated with the dynamically successful regions. That's not Berlin, not Luxembourg, not Brussels. It's Seoul, it's Manilla, and above all it's Beijing. China is the superpower of the future.

Over thirty years ago Hugh Gaitskell said that joining the Common Market would be the end of a thousand years of our history. Ladies and gentlemen, I call on you to vote for the start of the next thousand years. I second the motion. **9**

——— Speeches from the floor ———

Speeches from the floor are usually subject to a restrictive time limit, perhaps a couple of minutes or so. There is usually only time to make one or two points. It is better to make one point in a devastating manner than try and squeeze in a lot of different points. Here are some examples of points that could be made in the same debate about the European Union.

First point

❝ The proposer told us that he had a dream last night and that he talked to his grandfather. What a coincidence. I had a dream last night too, and I talked to my grandfather. He was killed in the First World War as well.

And grandfather asked me what life was like eighty years on. I told him that it was pretty good. I told him that there had not been a major war in Europe for more than half a century. I told him that all the former enemies were working together in a marvellous European Union. And I told him that this European Union had brought us all great prosperity. And I told him that I was just as British as he was.

And do you know what my grandfather said? He said 'Well done – don't let them throw it away'. I reckon that my grandfather was wiser than his grandfather. I am going to vote against the motion. ❞

Second point

❝ We have heard two views about how our partners would react if we pulled out. I am with those who say that they would react badly.

Why do I say that? Because it would be like a divorce. And nearly all divorces turn out to be bitter. I should know I've had one. It shouldn't be like that, but it usually is. And divorcing partners fight about everything, especially the furniture. And deserted partners try and get revenge.

If we do pull out, *beware*. It will be rough. ❞

Third point

❝ The proposer is very selective in his list of countries that manage well outside the European Union. I put it to you that Japan is a special case, a very special case.

What about Somalia? What about Romania? What about Patagonia? Do the goods of these countries sell well in Britain?

No they do not. I think that this is much more likely to be our experience.

I like the prosperity that we have and I do not want to risk it. I am against the motion. **9**

There are obviously hundreds of ways that a point from the floor can be made. However, the above examples illustrate some of the principles. They are short, sharp, imaginative, and make it clear on which side of the argument each speaker stands.

——— The summing up speech ———

The art of effective summing up is not easy to master. The speaker will be confronted by a mass of material, the majority of which must be ignored. He or she will be preparing under pressure whilst the other speeches are made. These other speeches continue until a few seconds before the summing up begins, and perhaps something from the last speech of all is worthy of comment.

Here are some techniques often used in a successful summing up.

- If the speakers from the floor have seemed to favour your side, comment on it and recognise the majority. Congratulate the speakers on their soundness. Of course, if they have favoured the other side you cannot do this.
- The summing up is a final chance to counter points made by the opposition. But do not spend too much time doing this, just mention one or two short sharp points.
- You should briefly restate some of the main points made for your side. Look to do this with a telling phrase, or somehow in a memorable way.
- Try to bring order and a theme into your summing up.
- End the summing up on a very strong positive note. This should be a point for your side, not a counter to a point from the other side. Perhaps you can find the key sentence that sums up the whole case.

Finally, on the following page is an example of a summing up of the case for the motion in the European Union Debate.

Specimen summing up speech for the motion 'This House Believes That Britain Should Withdraw From The European Union'

- **TIME** *2¹/₂–3 minutes*

❢ The vote may be close but we seem to have a majority of the speakers with us. Certainly in the quality of the arguments made, and I think in number too.

The main theme of the debate has been our loss of sovereignty. I thank you for all the examples and your accounts of the ridiculous bureaucracy. Some of them were very funny. I have not heard of the European standard condom, but I am prepared to believe it. And I am sorry for the Portuguese with their problems.

But whether this exists or not, there are hundreds of examples that are true. Let me confirm to the last speaker. We really do not have a free hand to make a law banning the export of live calves from Britain. It really has gone that far.

Trade is obviously very important and I am greatly encouraged by the confidence that many of you have expressed in our great future outside the European Union. There were many points made but I would like to mention just the one. Mrs Smith asked if they are suffering in Switzerland. I have just come back from there and I can tell you – no they are not. There is very little starvation on the streets of Zurich and Geneva. If fact I did not see a single casualty. They are managing pretty well without the European Union. And so will we.

Ladies and gentlemen, the clock is ticking and it is five minutes to midnight. It will soon be too late, but we still have the chance to take back control of our own destiny. We ask you to do that and support the motion. ❢

SUMMARY

1 Study the opening chapters of this book. You will need many of the techniques.

2 Check the content in advance with other members of your team.

3 Be aware of the time limit and other rules.

4 Counter the points of the opposition, but do not neglect to make your own points.

5 Help each other, but keep it simple.

6 Be persuasive. Probably use both logic and emotion. Aim for 'logic on fire'.

7 End both a speech and a summing up with a strong point for your side.

8 If speaking from the floor, make your point short, sharp and telling.

APPENDIX

—————— Useful addresses ——————

TOASTMASTERS INTERNATIONAL

Toastmasters International operates in most countries of the world.

Britain and Ireland
Mr M Silverman
11 Harvest lane
Gateacre Park
Thames Ditton
Surrey KT7 0NG
Business Tel: 0171 439 2717
Home Tel: 0181 339 0103

All Other Countries
Toastmasters International
PO Box 9052
Mission Viejo
CA 92690
USA
Tel: (714) 858 8255

THE ASSOCIATION OF SPEAKERS CLUBS

This organisation operates only in Britain. Contact address is:

Mr D Carlyle
National Development Officer
The Association of Speakers Clubs
60A Lansdowne Road
Bromley
Kent BR1 3PQ
Tel: 0181 460 0921

INDEX